A Jewish Child is Born

בריתי היתה אתו החיים והשלום:

My covenant was with him Life and Peace:

MALACHI 2:5

A Jewish Child is Born

The History and Ritual of Circumcision,
Redemption of Firstborn Son, Adoption, Conversion and
Choosing and Giving Names

by NATHAN GOTTLIEB

Bloch Publishing Company • **New York**

Library of Congress Card Catalog Number: 60-16833

SBN 0-8197-0017-7

PRINTED IN THE UNITED STATES OF AMERICA

to

Yerachmiel Gedalya

Esther Chaya Brachah

Melech Henoch

ז״ל

In memory of my beloved parents

RABBI MORDECAI AND ESTHER GOTTLIEB

of blessed memory
who kindled in me
the zeal for Jewish tradition
and religious observance.

Preface

Conformity to the *Din Torah* does not complete the calendar of Jewish duty. *Talmud Torah* is vital to a full Jewish life.

Im en deah havdalah minayin—for without knowledge there is no chance of distinguishing right from wrong. This applies in particular to *mitzvot ma'assiyot*, the so called ceremonial laws.

Into the vacuum of uninformed minds enter trivialities and superstitions, *telalim raim*.

It is our author's great merit to have shed light on many aspects of *Brit Milah*, to have brought home the combination of loyalty and common sense, of genuine devotion and happy humor, which render such occasions blissful. To his professional skill, Rabbi Gottlieb has added empathy, sympathy, the benefit of study, and the priceless ingredients of reverence, which enhance the significance of this volume.

LEO JUNG

Contents

Acknowledgments

My first expressions of gratitude are due my teacher and friend, Rabbi Dr. Morris Shoulson of Philadelphia for his encouragement and inspiration.

Rabbi Dr. Leo Jung, in addition to his preface, has given me the benefit of his scholarly counsel, while Rabbi Abraham Burstein made available his unique editorial experience and knowledge.

Rabbis Abraham Scheinberg and Jack Tauber are beloved colleagues whose erudition, assistance, and talents have been constantly at my disposal.

Rabbi Solomon Zeides helped me secure the many reference sources, while the suggestions of Rabbis Leon Katz, Arnold A. Lasker and Hershel Matt were gratefully incorporated.

Introduction

The insignificant number of books in English devoted to milah (ritual circumcision) deal with the theme in so technical a manner that they are not likely to hold the attention of the reader whose concern is not technical.

Written with American Jewish parents in mind, this book, by a rabbi who practices milah as a profession, is pointedly suited for such an audience. Rabbi Nathan Gottlieb's work is sure to fill the need of the American Jewish home for a reference manual on every prescribed religious ceremony from the first day of the baby's life to the thirty-first post-natal day. For it is during this period immediately after the arrival of the "bundle from heaven" that young parents usually ask most of the questions so adequately answered in this book.

Probably no other mitzvah was and is more consistently observed by the Jewish people as a whole than the practice of circumcision. At times, in many periods of our history, milah was practiced by our ancestors even at peril of their lives, because circumcision, like observance of our Sabbath and the study of Torah, was forbidden us by many tyrants under penalty of death.

Today milah persists and is universally observed by free Jews everywhere. An overwhelming majority of the world's population practices circumcision for one reason or another.

However, this very acceptance and popularity has led some otherwise well intentioned Jews to a false evaluation of this centuries-old religious observance, and to think that any physician — simply because he can do surgery — can perform the brit milah.

A careful perusal of this book will convince the reader that only a medically certified and rabinically accredited mohel can perform ritual circumcision (sign of the covenant) upon the new-born male in accordance with the Torah and time-honored tradition.

What is here suggested is not necessarily a hope that all physicians refrain from performing circumcisions. A religiously observant Jewish physician may perform this rite. We have a more modest and limited objective. The Jewish physician who himself turns to his own rabbi to perform the marriage ceremony of son or daughter, should realize that milah is not just another surgical procedure, but one of the three (Milah, Sabbath, Torah) fundamental observances of Judaism. Hence, anyone who otherwise does not feel himself called upon to perform other religious ceremonies should, similarly, not hold himself fit to perform the hallowed rite of brit milah, even where misinformed or misguided or unknowing young parents ask it of him or agree to let him do so.

The great majority of rabbis decline the dubious honor of participating in, and dignifying by their presence, the so called "doctor-made" brit. They do not like to name Jewish males in their synagogues in cases where the circumcision has not been traditionally performed by a mohel. Girl babies only are named, as soon after birth as is feasible. Boy babies receive their names at the time and place of their brit milah.

Where the services of a bona fide mohel are unavailable the advice of an ordained rabbi should be sought, because even then, the ritual of *hatofat dam* should be performed by a qualified mohel as soon as possible after the surgical operation.

The Jewish community is sure to remain indebted to Rabbi Gottlieb for the many fine expositions, which will in time become part and parcel again of the beautiful ceremonies attending the arrival of Jewish babies.

RABBI DR. MORRIS SHOULSON
Philadelphia, Pennsylvania
Erev Shavuot 5720 – תש״ך

"Mazal tov! A new baby boy has arrived! We are all happy for you."

There is no greater joy than parenthood. You are at the threshold of a great adventure, but there is also the concern for the little life that you now hold and must mold.

Nature endows our hearts with yearning to offer joyous gratitude to the Creator for his gift. Our religion bids us express our thanks by linking our boy with Him and His people — a cultural link which is both physical and a basis for mutual understanding. The performance of *brit milah* (ritual circumcision) is an ancient tradition. Through circumcision a Jewish male child is ushered into the covenant of Abraham.

It is my duty as a rabbi and mohel to explain the duties of Jewish parents to their newborn son.

At the rites prescribed for birth, marriage, and death, the three most significant experiences in our lives, we express our devotion to God.

Circumcision, according to the Bible, is a religious obligation, not a scientific principle. Since it concerns the first religious practice required of them when their son is born, Jewish parents are to re-enact the divine commandment of the "covenant of Abraham," given by God to Abraham for himself and his descendants, through every generation.

No one book or collection of books could encompass all the beauty and value of *brit milah*. It involves tradition and custom as well as medical and surgical procedure. We ought to understand this ceremony in its proper perspective, hence this volume.

Included are some traditional ceremonies for newborn babies, as well as some lesser known facts concerning them. I have incorporated their historical basis in Jewish law. Authority in the Jewish religion resides not in individuals but in the law as interpreted by the men who understand and believe in it.

All that concerns a Jewish male from the moment of his birth through the thirty-first day of his life, is here recorded.

NATHAN GOTTLIEB

Erev Pesaḥ 5720-1960

I

PREVIEW

~~~~~~

Little Jewish King

ARRANGEMENTS BEFORE AND AFTER

INVITATIONS

BRIT CLOTHING

FEAST

TIME

The Covenant Uniting
the Jewish Child
with his God
a Religious Obligation
of Jewish Parenthood

Little Jewish King

~~~~~~~~~~~~~~~~~~~~~~~~

ARRANGEMENTS BEFORE AND AFTER

Your first thought after the excitement has subsided is how to arrange for the *brit*.

Check the hospital's regulations pertaining to a brit when you make arrangements for the confinement. Policies and rules are set by hospitals regarding the recommendation of a mohel, physical facilities, the number of guests who may attend, and food allowed to be served.

Since every hospital has different facilities and requirements, embarrassing situations may thus be avoided.

Most hospitals submit a list of approved mohalim permitted to operate under their auspices who have a record of successful practice. If you do not know a mohel personally, you may inquire at the hospital or in your synagogue. If, for any reason, a deviation from the usual procedure is suggested, you should turn to a competent rabbi.

When you engage the mohel, he will inform you of the date, time and of the necessary accoutrements you will need. It is optional and just as effective to perform the brit at home, as in the hospital. These arrangements as well as

21

appointments of honor, the god-parents and sandek can be discussed with your mohel.

It is also necessary to inform the mohel if the parent (especially the father) is a Kohen, Levite or Israelite.

Last but not least is choosing the Hebrew name of the little boy prior to the ceremony. This eliminates last minute discussion and guarantees a happy ceremony.

INVITATION

After inquiring how many guests are permitted in the hospital (of course, if the brit is at home there is no limit), an invitation, with the date, time, and place, should be posted as soon as possible. The following is a standard form:

YOU ARE INVITED TO ATTEND THE

BRIT MILAH

OF

BABY_____

AT

(NAME OF HOSPITAL) _____

(Address of Hospital or Home) _____

DAY_____DATE_____TIME—————— AM
                                          PM

*(Signed)*_____

BRIT CLOTHING

There is no definite rule as to what the boy should wear on his great occasion. People generally expect that he will be in white, the color of purity. However, the only actual requirement is a suitable covering for his head.

CIRCUMCISION FEAST

At the conclusion of the ceremony the customary *seudat mitzvah* (religious feast) is usually held. The only essential item is kosher wine for the blessings.

A simple buffet of ḥallah, cake, fish, nahit (chick peas), and wine will adequately complete the festive portion of the celebration.

WINE

Kosher wine is needed at all Jewish festive occasions. The benediction is recited over wine, because of the scriptural statement, "Wine maketh merry the heart of man."

The prayer is recited after the circumcision, when the mohel gives the baby a drop of wine from the cup of blessing.

Wine brings happiness. We pray that the life of the newborn will be full to the brim with joy and sweetness.

TIME

A normal healthy child must be circumcised on the eighth day after his birth. This was practiced by our patriarchs even before the laws of Moses were proclaimed at Sinai.

The rite has been adhered to zealously and is so deeply ingrained in tradition that no postponement is permitted either for the *Sabbath* or the *Day of Atonement,* if it be the eighth day from the birth. It may be postponed only if the doctor pronounces the child physically unfit to be circumcised at that time, in which case the rite is performed at a later date — however, not on a Sabbath or a holyday.

Where there is a temperature elevation, conjunctivitis, vomiting, or similar disorder the halakhah (law) requires that a "normal" period of seven times twenty-four hours must go by; in more serious cases, thirty days; and in extreme instances, one is to be circumcised only as an adult.

Any circumcision performed before the eighth day is

not a ritual brit milah, and is contrary to biblical law
(Shulḥan Arukh. Yoreh Deah, Rema 264:3).

The brit milah is usually performed in the morning,
and if possible in the presence of a quorum of ten men (minyan). While the absence of a minyan is not necessarily a
deterrent, it is preferable that one be present.

If the child is delivered by Caesarean operation, the brit
may not be held on a Sabbath or holyday (Yoreh Deah
305:23 gloss).

If the child is born on Friday after sunset and before
the stars appear, the brit takes place on Sunday, if not a
holyday.

If it is doubtful whether the child was born while it was
still day, the eight days are counted from the following day;
if in such a case the eighth falls on Shabbat, brit milah is
postponed until the ninth day.

The exact hour of the baby's birth must be told to the
mohel, so that he can determine the day of the brit, because
we terminate the day at sunset when a new day begins. It is
the duty of the mohel to inform the parents that unless the
reason be other than the health of the child it is a violation
of a positive biblical law to perform the ceremony after the
eighth day.

II

CIRCUMCISION

Thou shalt keep my Covenant . . .

"Thou shalt keep My covenant,
thou, and thy seed after
thee in their generations. This
is My covenant which ye
shall keep between Me and
you and thy seed after thee"

Genesis XVII:9-10

Thou shalt keep my Covenant . . .

CIRCUMCISION

Practiced for some 4,000 years, circumcision is held in high esteem by all Jews. It is regarded all over the world as one of the basic rites of and a symbol of allegiance to Judaism.

There is no Jewish institution that is preserved more faithfully and accepted with greater joy than the rite of circumcision.

This universal law is mentioned three times in the Torah: Genesis: XVII:9-10-11-12; Exodus IV:25; Leviticus XII:3. "Every male among you shall be circumcised." "You shall be circumcised on the flesh of your foreskin." "An eight day old child shall be circumcised."

God spoke: *"I will keep in force my covenant between Myself and you and your seed after you as a covenant for all generations. You too must adhere to my covenant, you and your seed after you throughout their generations. And this is My covenant that you may preserve it: Let there be circumcised for you all males, and he who does not circumcise the foreskin of his flesh shall vanish from the circle of his people; he has destroyed my covenant"* (Genesis XVII: 14).

Thus spoke God to Abraham and thus he speaks to every descendant of Abraham. "Oh, youth, you who read these lines: Not in vain should you bear the seal of Abraham: Know you and know it forever: You are grandsons of Abraham, called upon to exalted tasks. May this knowledge fortify you in the battles you must fight. May it protect you and keep you from degradation. Let it be your pride to remain strong, faithful to the sacred convocation, symbolized in the name of Israel which you bear. Conduct yourself well at every moment before My countenance! Be pure and whole. Obey God with all that you are, with all the potencies that He has provided for you."

To maintain the purity of this covenant is to observe the whole Torah (ZOHAR GENESIS XIX:197a).

Short History of Circumcision

ABRAHAM

Jewish life began about four thousand years ago, with a great leader, Abraham. He was the first Hebrew to leave the tribe among whom he lived and travel to a new land. His departure parallels American life, which began with white immigrants to North America.

Abraham the patriarch ("a father who is also a ruler") chose the place where his tribe should live. For some time they lived in Babylonia, northwest of the Persian Gulf. Through this land runs a great river, the Euphrates. He could not travel to the east, because a strong people lived there who would not let him pass. Nor was it possible to travel to the west and south, for there the desert lay. He journeyed north and west till he came to Padan-aram. This new home did not satisfy Abraham. He wanted Canaan (Palestine). First, he hoped that with the help of God his tribe would grow into a great nation in a new land. Second, Abraham was anxious to find good pasture for his flocks of sheep and goats. Padan-aram was populated with many

Arameans, therefore lacking enough land and water for Abraham's flocks.

Palestine seemed rich in land, with plenty of room for his tribe. By crossing the Euphrates on his way to Canaan he earned for himself the name "Ivri" (Hebrew), which means, "One who comes from the other side of the river." This journey marked the beginning of Hebrew life.

The Hebrews began settling there at the beginning of the iron age, but circumcision goes back to the stone age.

In historical times Jews performed the operation with a stone implement. People are basically conservative in performing their religious rites and ceremonies. They were reluctant to change, hence the knife of polished stone was used even after the stone age. In course of time the steel knife replaced it.

God commanded Abraham and his posterity to give Him their soul and heart, *to be holy* in all their deeds according to His will. This was the first principle of the covenant God made with Abraham, and circumcision was a sign that Abraham was ready to comply with the will of God. He was the first Hebrew to be circumcised.

Before Abraham circumcised himself his name was Abram. After the circumcision it was God's wish that he become Abraham. This is the reason we name the child at the brit.

The rite involves highlights of history and biblical narrative. Three strangers (angels in disguise), tired and hungry, appeared before Abraham, who invited them to rest and eat with him. Thankful for this kind treatment, they promised that God would reward Abraham. His wife Sarah bore him a son they had long despaired of, and when the infant Isaac was eight days old the father, in token of the great covenant, performed upon him the rite of circumcision.

The older Isaac grew, the more dearly his parents loved

him. They felt he was more important to them than life itself. In those days many people thought they could show God their love by sacrificing their most beloved child. GENESIS XXII:1-2 reads: *"And it came to pass that God said unto him: Abraham, take now thy son, thine only son, whom thou lovest, even Isaac, and get thee unto the land of Moriah: and offer him there for a burnt-offering upon one of the mountains which I will tell thee of."* Abraham did as he was commanded. *"And Abraham stretched forth his hand, and took the knife to slay his son.* And the angel of the Lord called unto him out of heaven, and said, 'Lay not thy hand upon the lad.' "* All God wanted was his readiness to dedicate his son to Him. No human sacrifice was acceptable. Abraham understood that God was kind and good and did not want the sacrifice of little children. Jews always kept this story in mind, and never offered their children as sacrifices. Thus with Isaac the line was continued and the covenant confirmed.

DECREES ABOUT CIRCUMCISION

The Hebrews were slaves in Egypt, but they continued circumcision as a sign of submission to God. From the time the Lord made a covenant with Abraham, every Hebrew placed that sign on his body and on that of his sons.

Many times did tyrannical rulers try to abolish circumcision. The first was Antiochus the wicked, as it is written in the book of the Maccabees: *"And he commanded that they should not circumcise every male and each man who disobeyed the king's decree would be executed. And the women who circumcised their boys were executed according to the decree of the king"* (women also performed the operation). *"And they circumcised Jews who had not been circumcised before."* In the 23rd year of his reign, after reconstruction of the Temple, Antiochus came to Jerusalem with Bogros his aide and decreed the penalty of death for loyalty to Judaism. Circumcision, observance of the Sabbath and dietary laws, possession of Torah scrolls, became capital crimes. In forbidding circumcision and other rituals the enemy felt "that all would be one people." The Jew would lose his identity and become one of the mass. Though Antiochus had the land swarming with spies, his Jewish opponents were unnumbered.

Till this time, the precept of circumcision had not been broken except for the generation of the desert, which could not be cut and bled while on the way. The twelve tribes practiced it. The prophets never had to demand that the people be chastised for neglecting circumcision. There were some recalcitrants in the Babylonian exile, but all the sects that rose among the Israelites, such as the Samaritans and Sadducees, did not dare abolish the rite.

After the destruction of the Second Temple some rulers of Rome decreed the prohibition of circumcision; but during the days of the Maccabees, and ever after, when tyrants sought to destroy the Jewish faith by that prohibition, Jews zealously risked their lives for the right to continue their ritual.

The ancient Romans wished to destroy Judaism when they forbade the rite. During the Hadrianic persecutions (Bar Cochba Wars, 132-135 C.E.) Jews were not allowed to observe their rituals; but though detection spelt certain death, circumcision was faithfully observed.

Tradition has preserved in particular the memory of Eleazar, who died under torture for spurning the flesh of the swine, and of Hannah and her seven sons, all of whom perished for their faith, refusing to bow to heathen idols. Most outstanding was the devotion to the sacred precept of brit milah. Jews were always willing to sacrifice their lives in order to fulfill this commandment.

The Spanish King Sisibut ordered his Jews to accept baptism instead of circumcision (408 C.E.). Then they could remain in the land and have equal rights with Christian citizens. When the Jews heard of this they decreed a fast and wept openly. Many gentiles gathered to ask the cause of their grief. When told, they commented: "If you do not obey the king you will be compelled to abolish the entire Torah, therefore accept the little they ask for the sake of the many." But the Jews replied: "The precept of circumcision is the root of our religion. You say that he asks only a part. He asks us for all, and we will die ere we abolish this precept." They gathered before the king and said, "Hasten our death, for we will not give up a single law, especially one so important."

BIBLE

God spoke: *"Behold, My covenant is with thee, and thou shalt be the father of a multitude of nations . . . and I will make thee exceedingly fruitful, and I will make nations of thee, and kings shall come out of thee"* (GENESIS XVII:6). The future of your people is founded upon the sanctity of this covenant. As long as it is kept sacred, there will always remain loyal upright children to live in the spirit of the Lord.

Circumcision was enjoined at the age of eight days. It was applied not only to Abraham's descendants, but to all belonging to his household. The Bible addresses itself to the father, bidding him circumcise his child, significantly enough, not merely as father but as a representative of the family of Abraham. Every child is born into the family. In GENESIS XVII:14 the son himself is held accountable; his negligence is a denial of the covenant, and means forfeiture of his portion in the Abrahamic inheritance.

Being uncircumcised was considered a blemish. Circumcision was to remove it. It rendered Abraham and his descendants "perfect" (NEDARIM 31b; GENESIS R. XLVII).

Instances are recorded in the Bible where mothers performed this rite on their children. Zipporah, wife of Moses, circumcised her son Gershon by means of a sharp stone.

CUSTOMS AND CEREMONIES

Every act in the life of a Jewish child was governed by religious ceremonies and customs. Years ago he was not given the independence our children have today; instead, he was carefully nurtured and his early childhood was lived in a religious atmosphere, surrounded by the symbols and laws of our religion.

After the birth of the child, and as soon as the mother could walk again, she would repair to the synagogue, usually with the child in her arms, to offer her gratitude for God's gracious gift. This ceremony would include the rabbi's blessing mother and babe and the official welcome of the child into the sanctuary. Authority for this custom is traced to the Bible (LEVITICUS XII:6), and especially to the account of the birth of Samuel (I SAMUEL I:24), but until the fifteenth century it does not seem to have become prevalent; it was observed especially by the Jewish communities of Germany.

The first happening in a Jewish child's life after circumcision was to be placed in his crib; as part of a religious ceremony, the act required a quorum of ten (minyan). They set the child in the crib, dressed as he had been in the street procession to and from the synagogue. Then a Bible was placed on him, and all assembled called out, "May this child carry out all the commandments written in this book." They also set a quill in the infant's hand, as an omen that some day he would be privileged to write a *Sefer Torah* with his own hand. All present called out: "So shall it be."

This beautiful ceremony of the German and French Jews was later lost. The custom of placing the child in his crib, still prevails, but it is not a religious ceremony. In Eastern Europe, until of late, there were many who participated in the ceremony for the first time by putting sugar, raisins, cake, and even money into the crib "so that the child might have a sweet and rich life."

One of the oldest ceremonies connected with the birth of a child was that of planting a cedar to mark the birth of a boy, a pine or cypress to commemorate arrival of a girl. Besides being a reminder of the biblical comparison of a man to a tree (DEUTERONOMY XX:19), these trees would become useful when the babies, grown to adulthood, would stand side by side plighting their troth. From them would come the timber for erection of the *huppah* (canopy). Today, we plant trees in Israel in honor of the baby.

The Talmud records another interesting custom in conjunction with the child's growing up. Jewish mothers used to weigh their children, and the equivalent of each child's weight gain was given to charity. The Talmud also relates the story of Doeg ben Joseph, whose mother loved him so much that she made a daily donation to the Temple of the child's weight in gold. In Central Europe it is still customary to weigh the child on his birthday, and give charity in the amount of his gain. There were also Jewish mothers who pledged that after birth of their child they would bake a ḥallah for a poor family every Friday. If it was a boy, that would be done until his bar mitzvah, and if a girl, until her wedding.

Weaning was marked by a religious ceremony. In biblical times a feast was held, but later this ceremony was discontinued. The first solid food was taken from a stranger, in the hope that this should be the last time the child need receive anything from a stranger.

Noteworthy is the circumstance that in the Sephardic ritual the godfather and the sandek (the man holding the child during the brit) are one, while in the Ashkenazic they are the same only in certain countries.

Another practice was to hang a small bag around the child's neck, in which relatives and friends placed coins. This too signified that this might be the last time the child should receive gifts from other people.

Another ceremonial was the child's first haircut, for it was believed that his strength and life lay in his hair, and that cutting it at an early age deprived the child of health. Eastern European Jews believe the child's hair should not be cut before he can speak, for this will keep him from talking. The cutting of his hair at the age of three years was the occasion of a big feast. The honor of removing the first lock of hair was given the eldest guest, and if he happened to be a kohen, the honor would be even greater.

In some places it was customary to weigh the child's hair and give the equivalent weight in coins to the poor. In Israel when the child is four years old a ceremony is performed on Lag B'Omer. Many Jews from Safed and Tiberias cut their male children's hair for the first time on Lag B'Omer at the famous shrine of Rabbi Simeon ben Yoḥai near the village of Meron. This ceremonial coincides with the perennial pilgrimage of Jews throughout Israel on that day to the burial place of the reputed father of Jewish mysticism. There they sing and dance, and the child is dressed in his best. Other sections of the country also cut the hair on Lag B'Omer. Relatives and friends are invited, and everyone is given the honor of cutting a few hairs, until only the sidelocks are left. After the ceremony refreshments are served.

Among Sephardic Jews in Israel it is also customary to cut the hair for the first time during the intermediate days

of Passover. It is not done in the home, but in the synagogue, and they consider it a mitzvah for the barber. The
mother has made a pair of tzitzit for the boy and he has
been taught to pronounce the blessing and kiss the tzitzit
afterwards. He is also taught to say the morning blessing
by heart, and more blessings as he grows older.

When a little boy reached his first birthday it was a
custom of German Jews to bring him to the synagogue on
the Sabbath with a little Torah cover in his hand, inscribed
with his name and date of birth. In some European communities the "Wimpel" (swaddling clothes) used during the
circumcision was embroidered with his name and a Bible
verse. On the child's first birthday it was customary to present it to the synagogue, where it was used to cover the
Torah. The father was called up, and aferwards helped the
child put the cover on. The cantor or rabbi blessed the
child with the hope that he grow up in the spirit of Torah
and good deeds. In other countries the child was brought
to the synagogue as soon as he could walk.

Sephardic Jews observed this custom: when a child attended synagogue for the first time with his father, he do-
nated a waxed candle as a gift. Candles were kindled at the
brit, because it is written, *"The Jews had light and joy and
gladness and honor"* (ESTHER VIII:16; MEGILLAH 16b).
"Light and joy — joy means circumcision." An additional
Sabbath candle was lit for each child in the family. The first
two candles represented the parents. The customary practice of lighting candles at the brit is also traced back to the
years when anti-Semitic decrees prohibited circumcision.
The Jews were compelled to observe this rite in secret. To
notify their friends and neighbors that it was to take place,
they lit candles and ground spices and herbs, to announce
to the people in the area that they were invited. Although
we live in the United States, where freedom of religion is

the way of the land, we still carry out practices instituted many years ago. Many candles are used. Some light twelve candles, relating to the twelve tribes, and three large ones for the patriarchs, Abraham, Isaac, and Jacob.

To promote the Jewish education of children, it was good to take them to the synagogue, but it was not so good for the peace and quiet of the congregants. The Jews of Spain, however, found a remedy for this problem by placing the little children in a corner, with an older person to take care of them.

Gifts are also a custom. At the circumcision gifts are presented to the child, because the Lord gave the Holy Land to Abraham after the patriarch was circumcised.

Seventeenth century kabbalists introduced a custom still prevalent among East European Jews. The name of every Jewish child was associated with a scriptural verse, the first and last letters of which were identical with the letters of his (or her) name.

Three times daily, after the conclusion of the silent devotional prayer, the eighteen benedictions of the Shemoneh Esreh, the individual was to recall this verse. Legend has it that after death the soul must report to the angel of the grave, Dumah, and this verse would prevent him from forgetting his name at the hour of judgment.

If a child has more than one name, he or she repeats more than one verse. To illustrate this custom, a person named Tzvi (Hersch or its cognates) would recite, "Tzar umatzok m'tsa-uni mitzvotekha shaashuay"—"*Trouble and anguish have overtaken me, yet Thy commandments are my delight*" (PSALMS CXIX:143).

A girl named Zipporah (Feige or its cognates) would be associated with the verse, "Tziyon b'mishpat tipadeh v'shavehah bi'tzedakah" (ISAIAH I:27) — "*Zion shall be redeemed with justice, and they that return of her with righteouness.*"

The brit milah is the first occasion at which we pronounce the blessing, "L'Torah, l'huppah, ul'maassim
tovim." In every day life we often perform good deeds in
anticipation of a favorable return, to gain a good name or
special favor from God. The young child, who is the primary participant, has no ulterior motive in observing this
God-ordained commandment. We bless him therefore
abundantly.

כְּשֵׁם שֶׁנִּכְנַס לַבְּרִית כֵּן יִכָּנֵס לַתּוֹרָה וּלְחֻפָּה וּלְמַעֲשִׂים טוֹבִים.

K-SHEM SHE-NIKH-NAS LA-BRIT KEIN YI-KO-NAIS
L-TO-RAH L-HU-PPAH UL-MA-A-SSIM TO-VIM, that
he may participate in other happy events both spiritually
and physically; the ceremony serves as foundation for all
later actions to be motivated by noble ideals.

When the baby is brought in, the people say, *"Barukh
ha-ba"* בָּרוּךְ הַבָּא (Blessed be he that cometh in the name
of the Lord). The numerical value of the letters of *"haba"*
הַבָּא is eight, recalling that the brit has to be performed on
the eighth day.

The people knew that the education of a Jewish child
began at home — from the time he could see, hear, and
understand. Constant repetition of rituals and customs
rendered it second nature to participate in the traditional
way of life for him and his family, to become habituated to
the spiritual truths thus taught.

III

CEREMONY

Ushering the Child . . .

SHALOM ZAKHAR
CEREMONY OF THE BRIT
ELIJAH
PIDYON HA-BEN

Ushering the Child
into the World of Judaism
The Jew Expresses His Gaiety
in Prayer and Friendship

Ushering the Child into the World of Judaism

〰〰〰〰〰〰〰〰〰〰〰〰〰〰〰

שלום זכר

Shalom Zakhar

(Peace, Little Boy)

THE Jewish people have always felt an urge to share their happiness with others. While happy with any child, their joy was overwhelming when the offspring was a zakhar (male). A special ceremony expressed that delight: On the first Friday night after the birth, a party called Shalom Zakhar ("peace unto the son") is held in honor of the newborn son. People assemble at the home of the parents to recite psalms, sing songs, and discuss portions of the Torah *(Yoreh Deah* CCLXV, 12, gloss).

The following benediction is recited: *"The angel who hath redeemed me from all evil, bless the lads: and let my name be named in them, and the name of my fathers Abraham and Isaac; and let them grow into a multitude in the midst of the earth"* (GENESIS XLVIII:16).

The time has changed from the night prior to the brit; the SHALOM ZAKHAR is held on the Sabbath eve after

birth, because the Sabbath eve is a family evening, and
more guests can attend the ceremony. If the child was born
after the kindling of the Sabbath lights, it is held that very
Friday night (source: SHAKH, PERI MEGADIM, for the Sab
bath is known as SHALOM (peace), BABA KAMA 80a; TAZ,
MIDRASH RABA P. EMOR).

The original purpose may have been to prompt the
visitor to offer prayer on behalf of the new arrival and of
the mother. In course of time, folk lore suggested that the
prayers helped to banish the evil spirits lurking against those
confined to bed. This led to inclusion of many cryptic pas-
sages from the Zohar and other cabbalistic literature, and
advanced the sale of charms and amulets by adventuring ped-
lars. Needless to say, such unholy trade was looked on with
disfavor by rabbinic authorities.

Apart from this desire to share gladness with friends,
the reason for prayer and study in the room of the newborn babe may also have been psychological. Our ancient
teachers were firm believers in the value of attuning the
babe even in his cradle to the sounds of Hebrew, the
language of Torah.

When the celebration of the SHALOM ZAKHAR is
concluded and the guests are ready to depart, an honored
guest faces mother and infant as he chants the "Shema."

שְׁמַע יִשְׂרָאֵל, יְיָ אֱלֹהֵינוּ, יְיָ | אֶחָד:

בָּרוּךְ שֵׁם כְּבוֹד מַלְכוּתוֹ לְעוֹלָם וָעֶד:

וְאָהַבְתָּ אֵת יְיָ אֱלֹהֶיךָ בְּכָל לְבָבְךָ וּבְכָל נַפְשְׁךָ וּבְכָל מְאֹדֶךָ:
וְהָיוּ הַדְּבָרִים הָאֵלֶּה אֲשֶׁר אָנֹכִי מְצַוְּךָ הַיּוֹם עַל לְבָבֶךָ: וְשִׁנַּנְתָּם
לְבָנֶיךָ וְדִבַּרְתָּ בָּם בְּשִׁבְתְּךָ בְּבֵיתֶךָ וּבְלֶכְתְּךָ בַדֶּרֶךְ, וּבְשָׁכְבְּךָ
וּבְקוּמֶךָ: וּקְשַׁרְתָּם לְאוֹת עַל יָדֶךָ, וְהָיוּ לְטֹטָפֹת בֵּין עֵינֶיךָ:
וּכְתַבְתָּם עַל מְזֻזוֹת בֵּיתֶךָ וּבִשְׁעָרֶיךָ:

Hear O Israel

"Hear O Israel: The Lord our God, the Lord is One. Blessed be His name, whose glorious kingdom is for ever and ever. And thou shalt love the Lord thy God with all thy heart, and with all thy soul, and with all thy might. And these words, which I command thee this day, shall be upon thine heart; and thou shalt teach them diligently unto thy children, and shalt talk of them when thou sittest in thine house, and when thou walkest by the way, and when thou liest down, and when thou risest up. And thou shalt bind them for a sign upon thine hand, and they shall be for frontlets between thine eyes. And thou shalt write them upon the doorposts of thy house, and upon thy gates" (DEUTERONOMY VI:4-9).

SHALOM ZAKHAR thus offers a greeting of welcome to the blessed newcomer!

On the walls of the home hung these words: Text of PSALM CXXI:

מזל טוב לזכר

MAZAL TOV L'ZAKHAR

א שִׁיר לַמַּעֲלוֹת אֶשָּׂא עֵינַי אֶל הֶהָרִים מֵאַיִן יָבֹא עֶזְרִי: ב עֶזְרִי מֵעִם יְיָ עֹשֵׂה שָׁמַיִם וָאָרֶץ: ג אַל יִתֵּן לַמּוֹט רַגְלֶךָ אַל יָנוּם שֹׁמְרֶךָ: ד הִנֵּה לֹא יָנוּם וְלֹא יִישָׁן שׁוֹמֵר יִשְׂרָאֵל: ה יְיָ שֹׁמְרֶךָ יְיָ צִלְּךָ עַל יַד יְמִינֶךָ: ו יוֹמָם הַשֶּׁמֶשׁ לֹא יַכֶּכָּה וְיָרֵחַ בַּלָּיְלָה: ז יְיָ יִשְׁמָרְךָ מִכָּל רָע יִשְׁמֹר אֶת נַפְשֶׁךָ: ח יְיָ יִשְׁמָר צֵאתְךָ וּבוֹאֶךָ מֵעַתָּה וְעַד עוֹלָם:

"A Song of Degrees. I will lift up mine eyes unto the hills; From whence shall my help come? My help cometh from the Lord, who made heaven

and earth. He will not suffer thy foot to be moved;
He that keepeth Israel doth neither slumber nor
sleep. The Lord is thy keeper; the Lord is thy
shade upon thy right hand. The sun shall not
smite thee by day, nor the moon by night. The
Lord shall keep thee from all evil; He shall keep
thy soul. The Lord shall guard thy going out and
thy coming in, from this time forth and for ever."

The custom is being revived in this country, in our
own days.

סדר ברית מילה

The Welcome Ceremony

ברוך הבא

BARUKH HA'BA

(Blessed Be He That Cometh)

The brit is a happy occasion full of the beauty and
sanctity of Jewish tradition. It expresses the gratitude of
the parents to God for bestowing this gift of life on them,
and invokes His blessing upon the child.

The essential participants, in addition to the father and
mohel, are sandek and godparents (Gevatter and Gevatterin).
These are chosen separately and need not be married to one
another or be married at all.

SANDEK (the highest honor in the ceremony) is usually conferred upon the oldest or most pious and respected
member of the family, usually the baby's grandfather. The
sandek need not be a kohen.

The only other important requirement is a chair or
table known as the Chair of Elijah (kissai shel Eliyahu), and
kosher wine. It is a custom to have ten men, but this is not
absolutely essential.

The ceremony begins when the child is brought in by
the godmother. All present rise except the sandek, as the
baby is greeted by the mohel with the words בָּרוּךְ הַבָּא
(Blessed be he that cometh). The godmother hands the child
to the godfather. While the latter holds the infant, a prayer
is recited by the mohel:

אָמַר הַקָּדוֹשׁ בָּרוּךְ הוּא לְאַבְרָהָם אָבִינוּ הִתְהַלֵּךְ לְפָנַי וֶהְיֵה
תָמִים:

"God said unto Abraham, walk before Me and become perfect!" The godfather hands the baby to the sandek and the
baby is placed on the Chair of Elijah. The following words
are recited: .... זֶה הַכִּסֵּא שֶׁל אֵלִיָּהוּ זָכוּר לַטּוֹב. "This is
the throne of Elijah. May he be remembered for good" (PIR-
KE DE RABBI ELIEZER XXIX).

The mohel performs the ritual circumcision, recites a
blessing, then the father offers the following prayer:*

בָּרוּךְ אַתָּה יְיָ, אֱלֹהֵינוּ מֶלֶךְ הָעוֹלָם,
אֲשֶׁר קִדְּשָׁנוּ בְּמִצְוֹתָיו
וְצִוָּנוּ לְהַכְנִיסוֹ בִּבְרִיתוֹ שֶׁל אַבְרָהָם אָבִינוּ.

BA-RUKH A-TAH ADO-NOI ELO-HEI-NU ME-LEKH
HA-O-LAM, A-SHER KI-D'SHA-NU B-MITZ-VO-SAV,
V-TZI-VA-NU L-HAKH-NI-SO BIV-REE-SO SHEL AV-
RA-HAM A-VI-NU.

"Blessed art Thou, O Lord our God, King of the universe,
who hast sanctified us by Thy commandments, and hast
commanded us to enter our son into the covenant of Abraham our father."

All present recite the following:
כְּשֵׁם שֶׁנִּכְנַס לַבְּרִית כֵּן יִכָּנֵס לַתּוֹרָה וּלְחֻפָּה וּלְמַעֲשִׂים טוֹבִים.

K-SHEM SH-NIKH-NAS LA-BRIT KEIN YI-KO-NAIS
L-TO-RAH L-ḤUP-PAH UL-MA-AS-SIM TO-VIM.
"Even as he is entered into the covenant, so may he be led
to the Law, the nuptial canopy, and good deeds."

Another proud honor is called עֲמִידָה לִבְרָכוֹת
AMIDAH LI'BERAKHOT. After the circumcision a close
relative or friend may be honored with holding the baby
during the naming ceremony. The mohel or guest rabbi,
over a cup of wine, will recite the traditional prayers and
give the child his Hebrew name. A few drops of wine are
placed on the baby's lips. The cup used in the ceremony is
sent to the mother, that she may drink from it.

Then the child is brought back to his mother. She
says, "Mazal-tov; you are a little Jewish boy now," and the
ceremony is concluded.

The guests then join in a celebration called
סְעוּדַת מִצְוָה   SEUDAT MITZVAH.

At the conclusion of the SEUDAT MITZVAH the
בִּרְכַּת הַמָּזוֹן (Grace) is recited, and special prayers are
chanted for the good and welfare of the baby, father, mother,
and mohel.

תעודת ברית מילה
Certificate of Ritual Circumcision
This is to Certify That

_____
Son of

English	*name of father (*)*	*Hebrew*

English	*name of mother*	*Hebrew*

English	*date of birth*	*Hebrew*

WAS ENTERED INTO THE COVENANT OF ABRAHAM IN ACCORDANCE WITH JEWISH TRADITION AND THE LAWS OF BRIT MILAH

on the_____day of the Hebrew month of_____

in the year 57_____

At_____In_____

Hospital or home   City   State

The Name Bestowed Upon Him for Honor, Pride and Glory Is

_____
Hebrew name

May He Be a Blessing to His Parents, Relatives, To Israel and To Mankind

Godfather_____   _____

     Obstetrician

Godmother_____

Sandek_____   Guest Rabbi

_____

Amidah Liberakhot_____   Mohel

This boy became Bar Mitzvah on the_____day of the

month_____19_____at congregation_____

of_____

    city   state

(*) **Kohen** ☐ **Levi** ☐

ELIJAH THE PROPHET

Elijah is the personification of absolute faith. The prophet of redemption symbolizes implicit trust in the ultimate triumph of truth over falsehood. His zeal for God, devotion to Judaism, and insistence upon the spiritual and ethical values of Hebrew monotheism enthrone him as the living embodiment of Torah spirit.

When, under the influence of Jezebel, the king of Israel abolished circumcision in the Northern Kingdom (he himself abandoned this precept), Elijah retired to a cave. There he complained to God that Israel had forsaken the covenant of the Lord (I KINGS XIX:10-14). In consequence God "ordered him to be present at each circumcision," that he might witness Israel's loyalty.

The Talmud contains many stories of people who met, talked, and walked along the road with Elijah. Even dogs felt his approach to a city. People who recognized him made the most of their opportunity, asking the most important question they could think of, whether about their own salvation or some point of law.

STORIES ABOUT ELIJAH:

The prophet once met a man who sneered at holy things. "My son," said the sage quietly, "how wilt thou justify thyself before thy Father in heaven when He summons thee to swift and impartial judgment?"

"Oh, I know how to answer," the skeptic rejoined, unabashed. "I shall tell God that he ought to have given me knowledge and understanding, but as He did not, he is to blame, not I."

"What is thy business?" Elijah then asked.

"I am a fisherman."

"Thou art a fisherman," said Elijah, "and hast understanding enough to arrange nets, to hurl them into the water, to watch for fish at the proper time! Who gave thee understanding for this?"

"Understanding for all that sort of thing!" exclaimed the man. "Why, that is nothing. Every common fisherman has it."

"Nothing!" Elijah rejoined. "It is indeed something. Dost thou think much understanding is necessary to carry out the Law? The Law, says Moses, is near to thee; it is in thy mouth, and in thy heart, and thou canst do it."

Touched by Elijah's reproof, and convinced that the prophet had reason on his side, the fisherman wept tears of repentance and abandoned his skepticism (YALKUT SHIMONI, DEUTERONOMY XXX:14).

The story of the most famous of talmudic rabbis, Rabbi Akiba, illustrates his attitude toward women, as well as his love of learning. Rachel, the daughter of a wealthy landowner, Kalba Shebua, fell in love with her father's shepherd boy, and consented to be betrothed to him on condition that he study the Law. The marriage took place; but her father drove the husband away, and refused to help his daughter unless she leave him. So poor did they become that on one occasion she sold her hair to enable him to continue studying; their only furniture was a straw bed. One day a poor man called to beg some straw for his sick wife, and the shepherd gave him half of the bed, remarking to his wife, with the cheerfulness which never forsook him, "You see, there are some poorer than we." Fortunately, the poor man was the prophet Elijah, who still walks the earth, come to test him. Such things happened in those days (NEDARIM 50a).

CHAIR OF ELIJAH:

When a child is born his life is uncertain. We express our faith that God will protect him from physical and spiritual harm.

A symbolic chair is set aside for Elijah at the ceremony. Chairs specially made for this purpose are to be found in many synagogues. In central Europe they were generally double seats, one being reserved for the prophet while the infant was ceremonially placed on the other. Years ago the chair of Elijah stood proudly on its own in the synagogue where the brit was performed. No one could be seated in its place of honor. Frequently it was a handsome piece of furniture, property of the congregation, sent to the home as occasion arose.

BEFORE THE CIRCUMCISION:

The mohel takes the child, places him on the chair of Elijah. Elijah is the guardian of the little ones, and in this capacity is invited to the circumcision. "The angel of the covenant," he is called—MALAKH HABRIT.

ELIJAH'S CUP (Kos Shel Eliyahu):

The spirit of the prophet Elijah, harbinger of hope and redemption, is, according to Jewish tradition, present in every Jewish home on the seder night. Therefore, the service calls for a special cup of wine set aside for the prophet, as well as for a toast to his greatness, and for a prayer against the evil nations who refuse to acknowledge God and His just rule of the world. While this prayer is recited, the door is opened as a welcome to the prophet of universal peace and brotherhood. The glass of wine at the seder ceremony remains untouched during the service. Various explanations have been offered. It is best regarded as the glass ready for any stranger who might seek hospitality. Elijah is the prophet of redemption, and this, it is believed, will take place at Passover time. No guest is therefore more welcome than Elijah.

He appears as an old man, ready to help any one in trouble, such as children who have lost their way; sometimes merely a welcome guest, who comes unexpectedly, but answers no questions whence or whither. Tradition has ascribed to him the role of guardian angel over all who are weak and helpless.

פדיון הבן

Pidyon Ha-Ben

(Redemption Of the Firstborn Son)

PIDYON HA-BEN, Redemption of the Firstborn, is a rite observed by Jewish people when the first child is a boy. This ritual, which takes place on the thirty-first day of the boy's life, is one of the oldest in Hebrew tradition. It reaches back to the dawn of Jewish history, when the firstborn son was usually charged with the religious conduct of the household.

The PIDYON HA-BEN ceremony commemorates an important event in Jewish history. The culmination of Jewish redemption from Egyptian bondage was reached at the tenth plague. It is recorded in the Torah that after God visited the tenth plague on the Egyptians—slaying of the firstborn—all Israelite firstborn were consecrated to God. Because the Egyptian firstborn sons were smitten and the Jewish were saved, we redeem our firstborn sons through this ceremony.

Until the building of the tabernacle, the firstborn actually served as priests, musicians, and servants in the Temple. Consecration of the firstborn served to underscore one of the most important Judaic principles, that life is the most precious asset of the universe. In our holy Torah human sacrifices were severly condemned—especially the abominable practices of the heathen world, who slew their first male children in worshipping their idols. The Torah proclaimed the principle וָחַי בָּהֶם *"That thou shalt live by*

them" (LEVITICUS XVIII:5). All commandments were ordained for the purpose of promoting life. The Torah declared the firstborn sacred. He belongs to the holy Temple,
to be trained and guided towards the unfolding of his
potentialities.

The idea developed through the generations that the
first and the best belong to God. Firstborn males were to
devote themselves to the active service of God, while firstborn kosher animals were to be brought as offerings to the
Temple. So great was the reverence for life among the
early Hebrews that they would not use any firstling for
themselves. So too the first sheaf of wheat in the field, the
fruit of a tree bearing for the first season. The Bible contains the commandment: *"The Lord said to Moses: Con-
secrate to me all the firstborn; whatever is the first to open
the womb among the people of Israel, both of man and of
beast, is mine"* (EXODUS XIII:1-2). All firsts were offered to
God through the Temple.

The oldest son has always taken first rank in the family.
In case of the father's death, he usually became the head, to
whom the younger brothers and sisters looked for advice
and help. He inherited a larger share of the family's pos-
sessions than any of the others. In royal houses it is the oldest
son who usually ascends the throne upon the king's death.

As spiritual representative of the family, the firstborn
laid down the rules and regulations for the other children.
His example was followed. This explains the anxiety Jacob
displayed in securing the "birthright" from his brother
Esau. It was not material advantage he sought. He wanted
to continue the service of God which his own father consistently offered.

A child born to a father is not his absolute possession,
to treat as he pleases. It is a sacred charge entrusted to his
care.

Hence the remarkable question put to the father by the *kohen,* authorized representative of the Jewish faith: "Which wouldst thou rather, give me thy firstborn son, or redeem him for five selaim?" (This is equivalent to five silver dollars.) It sounds like a queer question. But the religious representative of the community must bring home to the father that he is to value his child more than his money. The father must "redeem" his child. That is, he must promise that he will receive the proper religious education and spiritual training, even though the father sees no immediate compensation for his parental sacrifices. This is the true significance of the law of Pidyon Ha-Ben. And because of his redemption, the firstborn son is charged with one duty that remains with him throughout his life.

סִיוּם בְּכוֹרִים -SIYUM BEKHORIM:

The custom of the firstborn son fasting on the day preceding Passover was a late gaonic innovation, to commemorate deliverance of the Israelite firstborn from the tenth plague (SOFERIM XX:3). To help the Jew observe his faith, this requirement was cancelled for the firstborn son who participated in a *SEUDAH SHEL MITZVAH.* Today, every synagogue has a ceremony observing the conclusion of study of a talmudic treatise *erev Pesaḥ* (Nissan 14 which is attended by firstborn males (or if they are very young, by their fathers). Participation in this precept, which ends with a collation, permits them to break the fast otherwise obligatory. Fulfillment of one positive precept (mitzvah) frees a person from observing another.

The rabbis of the Middle Ages did not especially favor continuation of redemption of the firstborn son after destruction of the Temple and cessation of the priestly functions. They could not abolish it. But they limited it by providing that the ceremony need not be performed if the mother too was daughter of a kohen or a Levite. This practice of redemption evidently proved a hardship on some families. Parents did not like to part with their oldest children. Therefore the tribe of Levi was set aside to act as priests and servants in the Temple, in place of the firstborn. In the Book of Numbers we read: "And I, behold, have taken the Levites instead of every firstborn; and the Levites shall be mine." Accordingly, every firstborn child was redeemed, that is, freed from service symbolically by paying the amount of five shekalim to the kohen or Levite who served him. It was after the Exodus that the duties of sanctuary worship were turned over to the kohanim, descendants of Aaron, and to the Levites, their assistants.

"And the Lord said unto Moses: "Number all the firstborn males of the children of Israel from a month old and upward" (NUMBERS III:40). It is like a man who had wares consisting of glass stones, and when he would bring them out to the marketplace he would pay no attention to their number, for he would not count them. When he put them back, he would still leave them uncounted, since they were made of glass. But he had one kind of merchandise which consisted of precious pearls, and these he would bring out by count and put back by count. For this reason it is written: *"Number all the firstborn males."*

The ceremony of redemption takes place when the child is thirty-one days old, even if for valid reasons he has not yet been circumcised. If the thirty-first day happens to fall on the Sabbath or a festival, the ceremony is postponed to the same evening or the following day. If for any reason the ceremony was omitted, the son has to redeem himself when he grows up.

סדר פדיון הבן

The Welcome Ceremony

A cup of wine and a ḥallah are placed on a table covered with a white cloth. Space is left for a pillow on which the baby is to lie during the service.

All guests participate in the following prayer, which is preceded by the washing of the hands and the blessing over the bread by the kohen:

בָּרוּךְ אַתָּה יְיָ, אֱלֹהֵינוּ מֶלֶךְ הָעוֹלָם,
הַמּוֹצִיא לֶחֶם מִן הָאָרֶץ.

BA-RUKH A-TAH ADO-NOI ELO-HEY-NU ME-LEKH HA-O-LAM HA-MO-TZI LE-ḤEM MIN HA-ARETZ.
"Blessed art Thou, O Lord our God, King of the universe, who bringest forth bread from the earth."

RABBI *(or kohen):*	Life comes from God, in whose image man is created.
GUESTS:	We thank the Lord for the gifts of this life.
RABBI *(kohen):*	The greatest joy is the joy of fulfilling God's commands.
GUESTS:	We rejoice in the privilege of taking part in this service.
RABBI *(kohen):*	Man and woman are partners with God in the miracle of bringing forth new life.
GUESTS:	We share the gratification felt by the father and mother.
RABBI *(kohen):*	God is served through learning and fulfillment of the Torah—through justice, reverence, loving kindness, faith, and humility.
GUESTS:	We dedicate this child to the service of God.
RABBI *(kohen):*	May the Lord help this child to grow up in health and with wisdom, and may the parents be blessed with the

physical and spiritual means of fulfilling their responsibility.

GUESTS: We pray for the welfare of this infant and his parents.

The father brings the child especially dressed for the occasion, and presents it to the kohen (who is presumed a lineal descendant of Aaron the high priest), and makes the following declaration:

זֶה בְּנִי בְכוֹרִי הוּא פֶּטֶר ‖ רֶחֶם לְאִמּוֹ: וְהַקָּדוֹשׁ בָּרוּךְ הוּא
צִוָּה לִפְדּוֹתוֹ. שֶׁנֶּאֱמַר וּפְדוּיָו מִבֶּן חֹדֶשׁ תִּפְדֶּה בְּעֶרְכְּךָ כֶּסֶף
חֲמֵשֶׁת שְׁקָלִים בְּשֶׁקֶל הַקֹּדֶשׁ עֶשְׂרִים גֵּרָה הוּא: וְנֶאֱמַר. קַדֶּשׁ־לִי
כָל־בְּכוֹר פֶּטֶר כָּל רֶחֶם בִּבְנֵי יִשְׂרָאֵל בָּאָדָם וּבַבְּהֵמָה לִי הוּא:

ZEH BE-NI BEKHORI PE-TER RE-ḤEM LE-IMO. VE-
HA-KA-DOSH BA-RUKH HU TZI-VAH LIF-DO-SO.
"This my firstborn son is the firstborn of his mother, and the Holy One, blessed be He, hath given command to redeem him."

The kohen then asks the father:

מַאי בָּעֵית טְפֵי לִתֵּן בִּנְךָ בְּכוֹרֶךָ שֶׁהוּא פֶּטֶר ‖ רֶחֶם לְאִמּוֹ
אוֹ בָּעֵית לִפְדּוֹתוֹ בְּעַד חָמֵשׁ סָלְעִים כִּדְמְחוּיַבְתָּ מִדְּאוֹרַיְתָא:

"Which wouldst thou rather, give me thy firstborn son, the firstborn of his mother, or redeem him for five selaim, which thou art bound to give according to law?"

And the father answers:

חָפֵץ אֲנִי לִפְדּוֹת אֶת־בְּנִי וְהֵילָךְ דְּמֵי פִדְיוֹנוֹ כִּדְמְחוּיַבְתִּי
מִדְּאוֹרַיְתָא.

ḤA-FEYTZ A-NI LIF-DOS ET BE-NI. VE-HEY-LEKH
DE-MEY FID-YO-NO KE-DIM-ḤU-YAV-TI MI-D'O-RAI-
SA.

"I desire rather to redeem my son, and here thou hast the value of his redemption." The kohen takes the money and returns the child to his father, whereupon the latter recites the following blessing:

בָּרוּךְ אַתָּה יְיָ, אֱלֹהֵינוּ מֶלֶךְ הָעוֹלָם,
אֲשֶׁר קִדְּשָׁנוּ בְּמִצְוֹתָיו
וְצִוָּנוּ עַל פִּדְיוֹן הַבֵּן.

BA-RUKH A-TAH ADO-NOI ELO-HEI-NU ME-LEKH HA-O-LAM A-SHER KI-D'SHA-NU BE-MITZ-VO-SAV VE-TZI-VA-NU AL PID-YON HA-BEN.
"Blessed art thou, O Lord our God, King of the universe, who hast commanded us concerning the redemption of the firstborn son."

בָּרוּךְ אַתָּה יְיָ, אֱלֹהֵינוּ מֶלֶךְ הָעוֹלָם,
שֶׁהֶחֱיָנוּ וְקִיְּמָנוּ וְהִגִּיעָנוּ
לַזְּמַן הַזֶּה.

BA-RUKH A-TAH ADO-NOI ELO-HEY-NU ME-LEKH HA-O-LAM SHE-HE-ḤE-YA-NU VE-KI-Y'MA-NU VE-HI-GI-A-NU LA-Z'MAN HA-ZEH.
"Blessed art Thou, O Lord our God, King of the universe, who has kept us in life and sustained us and enabled us to reach this joyous occasion."

The kohen takes the redemption money, and holding it over the head of the child, says:

זֶה תַּחַת זֶה. זֶה חִלּוּף זֶה. זֶה מָחוּל עַל זֶה. וְיִכָּנֵס זֶה הַבֵּן
לְחַיִּים לַתּוֹרָה וּלְיִרְאַת שָׁמָיִם. יְהִי רָצוֹן שֶׁכְּשֵׁם שֶׁנִּכְנַס
לַפִּדְיוֹן כֵּן יִכָּנֵס לַתּוֹרָה וּלְחֻפָּה וּלְמַעֲשִׂים טוֹבִים. אָמֵן.

"This is instead of that, this in commutation for that, this in remission for that. May this child enter into life, into the Torah, and the fear of heaven. May it be God's will that even as he has been admitted to redemption, so may he be led to Torah, the nuptial canopy, and good deeds. Amen."

The kohen places his hand upon the head of the child, and pronounces the following benediction:

יְשִׂימְךָ אֱלֹהִים כְּאֶפְרַיִם וְכִמְנַשֶּׁה. יְבָרֶכְךָ יְיָ וְיִשְׁמְרֶךָ. יָאֵר יְיָ פָּנָיו אֵלֶיךָ וִיחֻנֶּךָּ. יִשָּׂא יְיָ פָּנָיו אֵלֶיךָ וְיָשֵׂם לְךָ שָׁלוֹם.

"God make thee as Ephraim and Menasseh. The Lord bless thee, and keep thee. The Lord make His face shine upon thee, and be gracious unto thee. The Lord turn His face unto thee, and give thee peace."

יְיָ שׁוֹמְרֶךָ יְיָ צִלְּךָ עַל־יַד יְמִינֶךָ. כִּי אֹרֶךְ יָמִים וּשְׁנוֹת חַיִּים וְשָׁלוֹם יוֹסִיפוּ לָךְ. יְיָ יִשְׁמָרְךָ מִכָּל־רָע יִשְׁמוֹר אֶת־נַפְשֶׁךָ. יְיָ יִשְׁמָר־צֵאתְךָ וּבוֹאֶךָ מֵעַתָּה וְעַד עוֹלָם:

"The Lord is thy guardian: The Lord is thy shade upon thy right hand. For length of days, and years of life and peace, shall they add to thee. The Lord shall guard thee from all evil; He shall guard thy soul. Amen."
Both parents join in prayer:

"We acknowledge thee, our God and God of our fathers, as the source of all life's blessings. Thou hast created us and hast united us. Thou hast inspired our love and hast blessed our lives with our firstborn son."
All the guests present pray:

"May it be thy will, O our Father in heaven, that as this child has been privileged to undergo redemption, so may he be privileged to live in accordance with all the commands of the Torah. May he grow into manhood as a faithful Jew, conscious of his obligations, loyal to the traditions of his fathers, and dedicated to a life of honor, dignity, and good deeds. Amen."

The ceremony concludes with the blessing by the kohen, over the wine and is followed by refreshments.

בָּרוּךְ אַתָּה יְיָ, אֱלֹהֵינוּ מֶלֶךְ הָעוֹלָם,
בּוֹרֵא פְּרִי הַגָּפֶן.

BA-RUKH A-TAH ADO-NOI ELO-HEI-NU ME-LEKH
HA-O-LAM, BO-REI P-RI HA-GA-FEN.
"Blessed art thou, O Lord our God, King of the universe, who created the fruit of the vine."

The parents drink the wine, and the child is returned to his room. All the guests participate in the *seudat mitzvah* סְעוּדַת מִצְוָה.

At the conclusion, grace is recited. בִּרְכַּת הַמָּזוֹן

If the father is poor, it is the custom of the kohen to return the money after the ceremony, but it is not permissible to arrange for such return beforehand. If, however, the father is well off, it is the custom to select a kohen who is poor, so as to accomplish two good deeds at the same time—redemption and charity. The child must be actually a firstborn. If the mother gave birth to a daughter before the son, he requires no redemption. Only the firstborn son of the mother must be redeemed, but not of the father. If a man who has never before been married takes a woman who has had children by another husband, their firstborn son is not to be redeemed.

"Thou shalt take five shekels apiece by the poll" (NUMBERS III:47). The Holy One, praised be He, said: "You sold Rachel's firstborn, that is Joseph, for twenty pieces of silver, which are five shekels. Let therefore everyone of you redeem his firstborn son for five selaim, taking the Tyrian maneh as a standard coin."

There was a time when gold coin was used, but since 1933, when the United States went off the gold standard, silver coins have served the purpose.

The Torah declares the firstborn male child sacred, and the redemption a ceremony to honor him, home, and family.

תעודת פדיון הבן

*"Sanctify unto Me the firstborn males among the children
of Israel, for they are Mine . . .
At one month you shall redeem them . . . "*

This is to certify that

_____

Names of parents

HAVE FULFILLED THE MITZVAH OF

פדיון הבן
Pidyon Ha=Ben

REDEEMING THEIR SON, THEIR FIRSTBORN

_____   _____

English Name   Hebrew Name

As Commanded in the Torah

Grant that they rear him to be a true son of
Israel, firstborn people of the Lord, and a
faithful heir of the Kingdom of Priests, the
Holy Nation.

Father_____   Kohen_____

Mother_____   Rabbi_____

_____day of_____, 57   ____day of_____, 19___

IV

LAWS

He Who Teaches a Child is Regarded as His Father

SANHEDRIN 19b

LAWS
ADOPTION
CONVERSION

We Cannot Separate a Jew
from his Laws
or Much of Value
Will be Lost in the Process

IV

דיני מילה

He Who Teaches a Child is . . .

~~~~~~

LAWS PERTAINING TO CIRCUMCISION

1. It is a positive law for a father to circumcise his son, or to bestow the honor and appoint another Israelite to circumcise him. The father should stand near the mohel when the circumcision takes place, to indicate thereby that he is his agent.

2. It is customary for all those present at the circumcision to remain standing, for it is written: "And the people stood to the covenant" (II KINGS XXIII:3), with the exception of the sandek, who holds the child; he may remain seated. After the father has pronounced the benediction, those assembled say:
"As he entered into the covenant, so may he enter into study of the Torah, his nuptial canopy, and performance of good deeds."

3. Extreme care should be taken not to circumcise an infant who is ailing, as the fulfillment of all precepts must be postponed if there is danger to life. Moreover the circumcision can be performed later than the time appointed by Law. As soon as the child is eligible for circumcision it is forbidden to delay the performance for any reason, e.g.,

to gain time for providing the feast, or the like. But in case of a delay it should not be performed on the Sabbath or a festival.

4. When an infant is born at twilight or a little before, the rabbi should be consulted as to when he should be circumcised.

5. The ceremony is observed on the eighth day, even if it falls on the Sabbath or Yom Kippur, and can be postponed only on medical advice or if it is impossible to obtain the services of a mohel. But when performed at a later date, it can not take place on the Sabbath or festivals.

6. A male infant must not be circumcised without the father's knowledge.

7. A proselyte must, before he can enter the communion of Israel, be circumcised. If, while still a gentile, he had already been circumcised, it is requisite to draw a drop of blood from the membrum on the day he is received, as a sign of the covenant. The ritual bath (tevilah be-mikvah) completes the physical requirements.

8. Similarly, if the male infant is born with the prepuce absent, it is requisite to draw a drop of blood from the membrum, when the infant is eight days old.

9. Circumcisions are performed only during the daytime after sunrise, whether the operation takes place on the eighth day, the regular time, or subsequently, from the ninth day on, for it is said, "on the eighth day" (GENESIS XVII:12), i.e. by day, not by night. If the circumcision takes place after daybreak it is proper. The whole of the day is proper for circumcision. Still it is a duty to perform it in the early hours, for "the zealous fulfill their religious obligation at the earliest possible time."

10. If an infant is born when it is dusk and it be doubtful whether it is still day or already night, the eight days are counted from the night and the infant is circumcised on

the nominally ninth day, which may in effect be the eighth day after its birth. If an infant is born on the outgoing of the Sabbath at dusk, the circumcision does not override the obligation of observing the Sabbath. It is circumcised on the first day of the week, since it is doubtful whether the Sabbath is not superseded.

11. It is customary to make a feast consisting of fruits and beverages on the Sabbath eve preceding the day of the circumcision. This is considered a feast held in honor of the performance of a precept.

12. Whenever possible the circumcision should be performed in the presence of a quorum of ten adult persons; but when it is impossible, it may be performed in the presence of less than ten.

13. After the circumcision, it is customary to put a little wine into the mouth of the infant; then the verse *Bedamayikh Hayi* ("In thy blood thou shalt live") is repeated twice (EZEKIEL XVI:6).

14. If there are two infants to be circumcised, even if they are twin brothers, they shall first circumcise one and thereafter bring in the other, so that the benedictions can be pronounced for each one separately.

15. If a child is born circumcised it is necessary to draw a drop of blood (Hatofat Dam). This ritual must not be performed on the Sabbath or holyday.

16. If a mourner (even for his father or mother) be sandek, he is permitted to wear his Sabbath garments until after the circumcision; and join in the feast, after the first thirty days of mourning.

The above laws are found in SHULḤAN ARUKH, YOREH DEAH.

LAW AND CUSTOMS

1. There are a number of causes which delay the day of circumcision beyond the eighth day. The Mishnah states

that a child can be circumcised on the eighth, ninth, tenth,
eleventh, or twelfth day, but never earlier or later.

    a. Circumcision cannot be performed on the
eighth day (a child born at twilight is circumcised on the ninth day).

    b. The child born at twilight on the eve of the
Sabbath is circumcised on the tenth day.

    c. If the child is born at twilight on Sabbath
followed by a holyday, he is circumcised on
the eleventh day.

    d. If the child is born at twilight on a Sabbath
followed by the two day New Year, it is
circumcised on the twelfth (the two days of
Rosh Hashanah are regarded as one day of
holiness).

    e. A child who is ill may not be circumcised
until he is well. The circumcision is then
performed on the seventh day after complete
recovery (SABBATH 19 MISHNAH 5).

2. If the first of twin males is born on Friday at twilight, and the second after twilight (which is considered
night) the second child is circumcised on the following Sabbath, while the firstborn enters the covenant on the following
Sunday.

3. If a brit occurs on Friday, it is necessary to begin the
seudat mitzvah before two o'clock. If compelling reasons
prevent this, however, then the meal should take place immediately after Minḥah. When the Sabbath approaches and
the worshipers sanctify the holy day, it is customary to spread
a cloth to cover the festive table and proceed with the
Maariv service. It is not necessary to say grace prior to this,
because prayer is not considered an interruption (hefsek) of
the service.   BAYS ḤODESH

4. If a brit occurs on the New Moon (Rosh Ḥodesh) a special dish should be prepared in honor of the New Moon and placed on the table.

5. A brit that occurs on Purim should take place after the Scroll of Esther is read.   REMA

6. A brit that occurs on the day prior to Erev Pesaḥ (Passover Eve) should take place before the time allotted for the cleaning out of the hametz. If the brit was delayed until after that time, then food to be utilized for fulfillment of the mitzvah that evening must not be eaten at the festive meal associated with the brit.   RESPONSUM, NODA BIYEHUDA

7. If a brit takes place any time between the first day of the Hebrew calendar month Av and the ninth day of the month (Tishah B'Av) it is permitted to gather an exact minyan for the brit and they are allowed to eat meat and drink wine. In addition, the mohel, sandek, and father are permitted to cut their hair in honor of the occasion.
    ḤATAM SOFER ORAḤ ḤAYIM CCLVIII

8. If a brit occurs on the ninth day of Av, the father of the child is not permitted to eat despite the fact that to him the day of the brit is considered a holyday. The brit should take place upon completion of the reading of kinnot (Lamentations) after twelve o'clock. The father as well as the sandek and the mohel should don festive garments. According to some authorities they are even permitted to wear a tallis, which should be removed immediately after the brit. The festive meal should take place at night.   BRIT AVOT

9. There are some authorities who permit the father of the child, the sandek, and the mohel to eat immediately after the Minḥah services on a Tishah B'Av that has been

put ahead (nidḥah). This leniency, however, does not apply to a brit that takes place after the appointed time (eighth day).   YAABETZ

10. Even though it is customary to fast the day preceding Rosh Hashanah, this custom is set aside if it interferes with the festive meal of the brit. Those who are not active participants in the ceremony itself may refrain from eating if they so choose. However, the participants are required to partake of food.   MAGEN ABRAHAM

11. If a brit occurs on Rosh Hashanah, the circumcision should take place immediately preceding blowing of the ram's horn.   ELIYAHU RABBA

12. If a brit occurs on the fast day, Tzom Gedaliah, the father of the child is permitted to partake of food if he finds it difficult to fast the entire day. This may be allowed only if he waits till at least 12:30 P.M. and reads the Minḥah service first. This leniency is also accorded the mohel and the sandek, but not to the other participants.

13. If a brit occurs on the day before Yom Kippur, the circumcision and the festive meal should be held as early as possible. This should be done in order that there be adequate time for the meal eaten on the same day, prior to the advent of Yom Kippur, in honor of that holyday.

14. A brit that occurs on Yom Kippur should take place immediately after reading of the Torah. If the brit takes place outside the synagogue, it should be done after the scrolls of the Torah have been returned to the Ark. The blessings associated with the brit are rendered without the customary cup of wine. Other sages are of the opinion that the usual procedure may be followed, but that a little of the wine should be given the infant.

15. A brit that occurs on the day before Succot should be held as early as possible, as everyone is occupied with the preparation of the succah. The ceremony and meal should be concluded before noon of that day.

16. If a brit takes place in a synagogue on Hoshaanah Rabbah it is recommended that it be performed immediately before the Hosha-anot. This is done because in these prayers we beseech God's salvation by virtue of the merit of the brit (covenant).

17. It is customary for the parents not to select as sandek one who has already officiated as such. The honor should be given another.

18. It is customary to give the honor of Gvatter and Gvatterin (godparents) to an engaged couple.

דיני פדיון הבן

Laws Pertaining To Pidyon Ha-Ben

(Redemption Of Firstborn Son)

1. Every Israelite is duty bound to redeem his son, who is the mother's firstborn, from the kohen, by giving him five selaim, equivalent to about five silver dollars in our money. The kohen may be given other articles of value, but no real property and no notes may be given him.

2. If a miscarriage has occurred during the first forty days of pregnancy a Pidyon Ha-ben is still required, if a subsequent child should happen to be a boy. Should the miscarriage occur after forty days of conception, redemption is not required.

3. If on the day the redemption is to take place the father of the child cannot be present, it must take place nevertheless.*

4. The mother is not obliged to redeem her firstborn son; but if the father is deceased, it is the duty of the rabbis to redeem the child.

5. Kohanim and Levites are exempt from redeeming their firstborn sons. Even the firstborn son of the daughter of a kohen or of a Levite, married to an Israelite, is exempt from redemption.

6a. If the child is a firstborn son who needs a Pidyon Ha-ben, but the circumcision cannot take place before the thirty-first day, redemption is still required on the thirty-first day, even though the ritual circumcision did not take place.

b. If the Pidyon Ha-ben did not take place on the thirty-first day, and at a future date circumcision and Pidyon Ha-ben are to take place on the same day, circumcision precedes redemption.

c. If the circumcision and redemption are to take place on the thirty-first day after birth the redemption precedes circumcision (SIFTE KOHEN).

7. A firstborn son delivered by Caesarean section, need not be redeemed.

8. In the event that the father has violated this law and neglects to redeem his son, or if the father is deceased and the rabbis fail to redeem him, the son must redeem himself when of age, and he must on that occasion pronounce the benedictions: "Who hast bidden us to redeem the firstborn" and "Who hast kept us in life."

9. The firstborn may not be redeemed before he is fully thirty days old, and on the thirty-first day the redemption must take place, because the performance of a precept should not be delayed.

---

*HOWEVER, THE FATHER MUST GRANT PERMISSION TO THE KOHEN TO REDEEM THE CHILD.   (Shach, 305:10)

10. The rite of redemption may not be performed on the Sabbath or on the festivals, but may be performed on the intermediate days of festivals (ḥol-hamoed).

11. If the day of redemption occurs on the Sabbath or on a festival, or on a fast-day, the rite of redemption should be performed at the conclusion of said Sabbath, festival, or fast-day.

12. It is the prevailing custom to perform the rite of redemption in the daytime. Nevertheless, if the thirty-first day has passed and the infant was not redeemed, the redemption must take place as soon as possible.

13. First the hands are washed for the repast, the benediction is pronounced by the kohen upon breaking bread, and then the ceremony of redemption is performed.

14. After the kohen has received the five selaim, he may return either the whole of it or a part thereof to the father of the infant; in either event the firstborn is considered legally redeemed. But he who desires to perform the precept of redemption as is required by law, should choose a kohen who is poor, learned in the Law, and God-fearing, and both the father and the kohen should resolve not to make restitution of the redemption money.

15. It is a meritorious deed to provide a repast at the ceremony of redeeming the firstborn.

16. The son of a lay Israelite woman married to a non-Jew must redeem himself upon reaching his majority. The son of the daughter of a Levite married to a non-Jew is exempt from redemption. The son of the daughter of a kohen married to a non-Jew must redeem himself upon reaching his majority, because his mother lost her priestly status through her marriage to a non-Jew.

17. An adopted child born of a Jewish mother, not of priestly or levitical descent, requires a Pidyon Ha-ben.

18. A boy born after his mother's conversion to Judaism requires a Pidyon Ha-ben.

The above laws are found in Shulḥan Arukh, Yoreh Deah.

ADOPTION

(Whoever brings one near to God is as though he had created him)

According to Jewish law the child's religion is determined entirely from the natural mother's status.

We determine the child's religion by his mother's religion. If the mother is Jewish (even though the father is not) the child is Jewish. The child of a Jewish father and a non-Jewish mother is not considered Jewish (KIDDUSHIN 68B) until converted.

This is a talmudic statement. "Rabbi Joḥanan said on the authority of Rabbi Simeon ben Joḥai: Scripture saith: *For he will turn away the son from following me* — this refers to a son by an Israelite woman—such is called thy son. But thy son by a heathen woman is not called thy son" (KETUBOTH 11a). An adopted child whose natural mother is non-Jewish does not fulfill all the requirements for proselytism merely by circumcision (a rabbi should be consulted).

If the brit is to be conducted *with the entire ritual,* it is of utmost importance that the mohel be informed if the mother of the newborn baby boy is not of the Jewish faith.*
If such is the case, the following procedure is required by Jewish law. The circumcision must be witnessed by a court of three rabbis or three laymen (Beth Din).

The mohel is one of the quorum. These men are witnesses that the circumcision ritual is being performed for the purpose of conversion (YOREH DEAH 263.5 *gloss).* The fact that the child was circumcised by a mohel with the witnesses present in itself does not make him a member of the faith. It is necessary at a future date, when the child is three years of age or older, that he be taken to the ritualarium (mikvah) and immersed in the presence of a quorum of three rabbis or laymen.

---

*TO BE CERTAIN NO FORBIDDEN MARRIAGE MAY TAKE PLACE IN LATER YEARS, IT IS IMPERATIVE THAT THOSE WHO ADOPT THE CHILD OF A JEWISH MOTHER BE APPRISED OF THE MOTHER'S HEBREW NAME.

If the adopted boy was circumcised (not by a mohel) prior to the adoption, in order to make a covenant with God, drawing of a drop of blood becomes necessary. When he has immersed himself and ascended from the water he is an Israelite in every respect.

Examples of Adoptions:

When the father and mother of Esther died, Mordecai "took her for his own daughter" (ESTHER XVII:7). According to Josephus, Abraham, while yet childless, adopted his nephew Lot (ANTIQUITIES, BOOK I, CHAP. 7, SECTION I). There was a widespread tradition that Bithiah, daughter of Pharaoh, adopted Moses (PHILO, LIFE OF MOSES, I:5; JOSEPHUS, ANTIQUITIES, BOOK 2, CHAP. 9, SECTION 7; MEGILLAH 13a).

A procedure akin to adoption was the case when a barren wife gave her handmaid to her husband as a concubine and reared the latter's child as her own (GENESIS XVI:2, XXX:3-6), or when a man with no sons would marry his daughters to his freed slaves (I CHRONICLES I:34-35). The idea of the levirate marriage is somewhat similar to adoption, since in this instance the childless widow is taken in marriage by the brother-in-law, and the children bear the name and inherit the estate of the deceased (DEUTERONOMY XXVI:5-6).

The probable reason that adoption was so rare among the ancient Jews was that they did not find it necessary to resort to such practices for lack of children of their own. The fact that polygamy was not prohibited and freedom of divorce and remarriage made it very unlikely that they would remain childless.

The rabbis declared that "whoever rears an orphan in his home is deemed by the scriptures as his parent." Among other proofs they instance the passage in which Obed is called the son of Naomi (RUTH IV:17). Whereas Ruth was his real mother, Naomi had reared him. Rabbi Samuel bar

Nahmani refers the passage *"happy are they who do right-eousness at all times"* (PSALM CVI:3) to those who assume the responsibility of rearing orphans and attending to their welfare. Abaye, orphaned at birth, was adopted and instructed by his uncle, Rabbah bar Naḥmani, and is frequently called Naḥmani in his honor (ERUBIN 29b, GITTIN 67b SHABBAT 66b). It was considered a privilege to be able to grant the proper education and upbringing to parentless boys of unusual ability and promise. "He who learns from his fellow a single chapter, a single rule, a single verse, a single expression, or even a single letter, ought to pay Him honor; for so we find with David, King of Israel, who learned only two things from Ahitophel, and yet regarded him as his master" (ABOT: SAYINGS OF THE FATHERS VI:3).

Voluntary acceptance of a child of other parents rendered him the same as one's own child. The legal concept of adoption finds no place whatsoever in biblical or talmudic jurisprudence. The Hebrew term AMETZ is a modern expression of this concept. However, although Jewish law did not formally recognize the institution of adoption, there were instances of voluntary assumption of parental care over another's child, even in earliest times.

When the adopted child is a female the same law exists of the natural mother's Jewish status. If the child does not have the Jewish birthright, immersion is required for her to become Jewish, and at the conclusion of the ceremony she is given her Hebrew name.

The mohel presents a certificate to the new parents which reads as follows: "I have this day circumcised this child according to the direction of the Beth Din, in accord with all precepts, rituals and requirements of the Jewish faith, and upon the explicit condition that at the proper time the child will undergo immersion in a kosher ritualarium, as prescribed by the Jewish tenets."

In modern times, when adoption has become more frequent among the Jews, various organizations have been formed in the larger cities to promote and supervise the adoption of Jewish orphans into Jewish families.

CONVERSION

Requirements for conversion to the Jewish faith are circumcision, immersion (mikvah), and acceptance of Torah precepts (YEBAMOT 47a AND JER. ZEBAḤIM 2:3). These are matters requiring consultation with an ordained rabbi.

A quorum of three rabbis or three laymen is required by Jewish law for the reception of the would-be convert (YEBAMOT 46b YOREH DEAH 268:3). The Talmud YEBAMOT 47a AND b states that the rabbi must make it clear to the proselyte that his becoming a Jew will unite him to a people and community perenially persecuted, and that he will be obligated to observe many laws from which, whilst a gentile, he is free.

1. The candidate for conversion must prove to the satisfaction of the Bet Din that no ulterior motive (like love of a Jewish person whom he or she wants to marry) prompted his petition for admission to Judaism.

2. The convert must make the most solemn avowal of his determination to obey Jewish law.

3. It is easier to admit him, when the Jewish friend himself or herself loyally lives according to the Din Torah.

Rav, one of the great scholars of the Talmud, says: "They must be received in friendliness, for it may be that they are converting out of sincere love of God." Those who are candidates for Judaism present themselves as proselytes and are instructed in the doctrines and observances of Judaism. When the convert is deemed to have received adequate instruction, he is ready to be circumcised by a mohel (YOREH DEAH 263:5 *gloss*).

The circumcision, says one author, is the seal of the will of God, a duty of the children of Abraham and also of the stranger who accepts the Jewish faith. Only by circumcision were strangers permitted to enjoy all the rights of the land and nation of Israel.

After the circumcision is healed the candidate for conversion is taken to the (mikvah) ritual pool in the presence of three male witnesses; after the immersion he is given the name Abraham. He is an Israelite. A woman proselyte is given instruction in law and customs and some of the commandments; she is then taken to the ritual pool to be immersed. "When they have immersed themselves and ascended from the water they are considered Israelites in every respect" (YEBAMOT 47a,b). The most famous advocate of friendly treatment of non-Jews was Hillel, whose rule was: "Be of the disciples of Aaron, loving peace and pursuing peace, loving your fellow creatures and drawing them near to the Torah" (ABOTH I:12).

The story is told that a heathen came to Shammai to be accepted as a convert, on condition that he be taught the whole of the Torah while standing on one foot. The rabbi drove him off with a yardstick. He then went to Hillel with the same request; and Hillel said: "What is hateful to yourself, do not do to your fellowman. That is the whole of the Torah; the remainder is but commentary. Go learn it" (SHABBAT 31a).

The following blessing is said at the conclusion of the conversion.

> May He who blessed our father Abraham, the first convert from paganism, to whom He said, "Walk thou before Me, and be thou perfect, and I will establish my covenant between Me and thee," bless, strengthen, and encourage the righteous convert, who has come to find protection under the wings of the God of Israel. He has

sealed the sign of the holy covenant on his flesh; he has been purified in the ritual waters; he has attached himself to God, to love Him and to serve Him. And this day he has been called for the first time to the holy Torah which God gave us through Moses. His name in Israel shall be (give Jewish name) son of Abraham. "May the earth be filled with the understanding of God, as the waters fill the ocean bed." "And the Lord shall be king over all the earth; on that day shall the Lord be one, and His name one." With the grace of God, Amen.

A certificate is given to verify that the candidate has been accepted into the Jewish fold.

תעודת גירות
(זכר)

אנו הח״מ מעידים איך שהמוכ״ז מר . . . .
בא לפנינו והביע את רצונו הטוב להסתפח לעם ישראל
ולחסות תחת כנפי השכינה ואחרי שדברנו אתו בדבר
ד׳ בהלכות והליכות של חיי ישראל ודיני ומנהגי
ישראל

ומצאנו שידועים לו עיקרי אמונתנו ותורתנו הק׳
קבלנו אותו לקהל ישראל אחרי שנימול — — — וטבל
בקבלת מצוות בפני ב״ד של שלושה

ומהיום והלאה יש לו דין ישראל לכל דבר ויקרא שמו
בישראל — אברהם בן אברהם

ועל זה באנו על החתום ביום ..... לחודש ..... בשנת .....
חמשת אלפים ושבע מאות .....
לב״ע למנין שאנו מונין כאן

נאום ....
נאום ....
נאום ....

Certificate of Conversion

(Male)

We, the undersigned, do herewith
certify that_____appeared before
us and declared his intention of joining
the Jewish people and assuming responsibility for the principles of our sacred
faith, according to the Torah (Law) of
Israel. Furthermore, for the purposes of
conversion, he has been circumcised and
immersed in the ritual waters of
purification, and accepted the sacred
precepts in the presence of a Beth Din,
a tribunal of three.

Therefore do we formally receive and
welcome him into the Congregation of
Israel and declare that he shall be
regarded as a complete Jew in all matters
of our faith and that his name will be
known in Israel as_____the
son of Abraham: and may it bring pride
and glory unto Israel.

In witness thereof we have here
placed our signatures this_____day of
_____57_____which corresponds to_____
day of_____19_____, in the city of
_____state of_____.

signature_____

signature_____

signature_____

תעודת גירות

(נקבה)

אנו הח״מ מעידים בזה איך שהמוכ״ז גברת ....
באה לפנינו והביעה את רצונה הטוב להסתפח להאומה
העברית ולחסות תחת כנפי השכינה.
בדקנו אחרי׳ ודברנו אתה בהלכות והליכות של חיי
ישראל ודיני ישראל המוטלות על בנות ישראל וביחוד
בדיני כשרות וטהרת המשפחה
ומצאנו שידועים לה עיקרי אמונתינו ותורתנו הק׳
והטבילה וקבלת מצוות היתה כדת וכדין של תורה
בפני ב״ד של שלושה
לכך אנו מקבלים אותה להמנות בתוך בנות ישראל
ואומרים לה אחותנו את — היי ברוכה כרחל ולאה
אשר בנו שתיהן את בית ישראל
ומהיום והלאה יקרא שמה בישראל .... ועל זה באנו
על החתום ביום ..... לחודש ..... בשנת ... חמשת אלפים
ושבע מאות ..... לב״ע למנין שאנו מונין כאן

נאום ....

נאום ....

נאום ....

Certificate of Conversion

(Female)

We, the undersigned, do hereby certify
that_____has come
before us and declared her intention of
joining the Jewish people and assuming
the responsibilities of Judaism; and
having ascertained that the principles
of our faith and ritual are known unto
her and that she has been immersed in
the ritual waters of purification for the
purpose of conversion before this
tribunal, as well as having accepted the
principles of faith according to the
laws and rites of Judaism; therefore do
we welcome her into the fold among the
righteous proselytes, and from this day
on she shall be known in Israel as
_____daughter of Abraham.
In witness thereof we have here
placed our signatures this_____day of
_____57_____which corresponds to_____
day of_____19_____, in the city of
_____state of_____.

signature_____

signature_____

signature_____

V

MEANING

Circumcision — A Bond with Antiquity

BINDING FAITH
MORAL PERFECTION
SYMBOL OF ALLEGIANCE

Trees Grow, Spread Their Leaves in Splendor;
They Wither in the Autumn and are no more;
Still the Tree Remains.

Man Grows in Strength, Purpose, and Mind:
His Beauty Shines From His
Acceptance of the Lord Our God.
Then Man Withers and is no More.
He Shines in Beauty
Through His Descendants

V

Circumcision — A Bond with Antiquity

~~~~~~~~~~~~~~~~~~~~~~~~~~~~~~~~~~~~~~~

BINDING FAITH
(Tradition and Experience)

THE Jewish people have rarely been fortunate enough to sink their roots long into one place. Too often have they been forced to wander the roads of the world. They have faced constant shame and persecution in almost every country and in all generations.

Without a country of their own, and no protection, they developed a feeling of political and social insecurity, but they never lost their ethical cultural identity, and they found comfort in devotion to their faith. It is an unparalleled historical phenomenon that for four thousand years the children of Israel have maintained a culture and tradition only because they never forsook their religious rituals.

If we let go of one ceremony and then another, we will soon find there is nothing left. Physically a mother is separated from the child, but the spiritual separation is never complete. Therefore, just as the mother cannot be separated from her child completely, we cannot separate a Jew from laws of the holy Torah. The factors which unite us are developed from the first day of birth.

(1) Culture (traditional). Our culture encircles us like an invisible shell; we cannot touch it. It enters our

blood stream. We are unaware at the time, but gradually the portrait becomes visible, the composite portrait of the Jewish people.

(2) Rabbi (experience). The rabbis of old who compiled the Talmud and Midrash were neither pedants nor closet scholars. They were down to earth teachers of people, robust with the life urge and endowed with good practical sense.

Their realism derived from the school of life. The universal duty to study as a religious act broadened the base of Jewish culture and elevated it.

The commandment of circumcision as written in the Torah four thousand years ago is old according to time, but still operative in our modern era and accepted as new. The combination of tradition and experience presents a problem almost as old as man himself, who remembers the past, but lives in the present. The issue is the conflict between the accepted tradition of the group and personal experience of the individual.

1. How can Judaism be preserved?
Survival is the result of laws, customs and traditions.

2. Can I be a good Jew without obeying the laws?
A series of laws exist. They can be traced to their source. Enforcement is purely voluntary, and each individual must decide for himself whether to follow or neglect them. An intelligent person is one who reads and listens and then decides after he knows what the subject matter is about. It follows that when men are no longer free to study the results of their immemorial teachings, even occasionally to find the ideas at variance with authority, a great conserving force in society has been lost. Repression of an idea does not disprove it.

"The only way to handle ideas is to permit them to be expressed and to expose them to the objective challenges of thinking men who themselves represent many diverse points of view."

(ARTHUR F. NICHOLSON, *N.E.A. Journal*)

3. *What harm do I do when I disregard the laws?*

There are many Jews who are proud of their religion but disregard the laws. Some unfortunately have not been trained in the tradition, others have discarded all symbols and rites, but without concrete forms and actions you cannot transmit the heritage to your followers. For they cannot read your invisible thoughts and the good intention is lost in oblivion.

4. *Is circumcision a tribal mark?*

Circumcision with the Jews is a sign of being servants to the Lord. The man who lives with His laws will impute great value to them. The law of circumcision implies compliance with the will of our Lord, therefore it is impossible to compare this servitude with subjugation to a ruler. The one who is subjected will comply with the will of his ruler, but his heart will not be in it.

5. *Do we become Jewish when we are circumcised?*

Judaism considers the rite of circumcision an external symbol binding the child to his faith. It is not a sacrament which inducts the infant into Judaism; his birth does that. Circumcision confirms the child's status and represents a mark of loyalty to the faith of Israel.

6. *Is it true that circumcision purifies sex morals?*

It is significant that whereas God endorses every act of the creation with the refrain "and it was good," he omits this recommendation when man arises—"a living soul" from the dust of earth, pulsating with "the spirit of God" breathing within him. Maimonides, who attempts rationally to explain many of the commandments beyond our ken, is of the opinion that this act contributes towards moral and sexual purity, a view already proclaimed by Philo of Alexandria more than a thousand years before. Be that as it may, it is not the hygienic aspect that is stressed by Judaism, but the religious, i.e., the spiritual and moral.

MORAL PERFECTION

Only among the Jewish people is circumcision a wholly religious rite between God and man, serving as a force for the survival of the Jewish family and the peoplehood of Israel.

In talmudic and rabbinic Judaism circumcision is recognized as based on ancient tradition and religious law. It has been interpreted as a symbol of the Jewish ideal of moral perfection and holiness.

The act is fulfilled only if and when it becomes a symbol, to be understood and appreciated as a living idea. Circumcision has been a distinguishing sign of Judaism since the days of antiquity.

With circumcision the child is made a Jew forever. He is taught to lead a good life. He must perfect himself. Through circumcision the newly born are dedicated to God, to His Torah, and to the highest moral and ethical code.

"Thou hast increased the nation, O Lord, Thou hast increased the nation: Thou art glorified." When God gives a son, the father circumcises him in eight days; if he be a firstborn, he redeems him; when the son is grown, he takes him to the synagogue, where he daily utters, "Praise ye the Lord." "Thou givest him a house, he affixes the mezuzah to it; a roof, he makes a railing around it to prevent falling off, thus protecting the stranger" (YALKUT TAZRIA).

SYMBOL OF ALLEGIANCE

The very name describes the importance of the rite to our people. BRIT means covenant or agreement, signifying that the Jewish people have accepted certain beliefs, laws, and ideals.

Circumcision's great value lies in the high spiritual concept of the rite. The Jew sees it as symbol of a covenant which every male individual in Israel enters into with God, and as expression of the devotion of the individual to his people. It has thus served as one of the great forces for the survival of Israel. Even the heretic Benedict Spinoza (1632-1677) declared: "Such great importance do I attach to the sign of the covenant, that I am persuaded it is sufficient by itself to maintain the separate existence of the nation forever."

The rite of milah is intended to glorify the soul and mind of the child, through the "covenant of Abraham."

The old seal of the covenant between Abraham and his Creator is a symbol of lasting faith, of the consecration of the children of Abraham to the God of Abraham. Jewish men and women have in all ages been ready to lay down their lives in its observance. The Maccabean martyrs died for it. The officers of King Antiochus, the Chronicler tells us, put to death the mothers who initiated their children into the covenant—"And they hanged their babes about their necks" (I MACCABEES I, 61). We find the same readiness for self-immolation when the Roman Emperor Hadrian aimed at destruction of Judaism; when in the dread days of the Inquisition obedience to this command meant certain death; whenever and wherever tyrants undertook to uproot the Jewish faith.

Instances of opposition to circumcision arose. In Frankfort, a Reform society came into existence which displayed even greater boldness. It proclaimed the Mosaic religion subject to unrestricted development, rejected the authority of the Talmud, renounced the hope of national restoration, questioned the validity of the dietary laws, and even denied that the rite of circumcision was binding. The last denial aroused too much opposition, and was dropped from the society's program. But circumcision remained a hotly debated issue, although nearly all the religious leaders, in Italy and Austria as well as in Germany, agreed that circumcision for the born Jew remained a part of Reform practice.

Today, when many of the old customs have been abandoned by many segments of our people, brit milah retains its hallowed place in its universal acceptance. Deviation from law is not the unity which the Jewish structure has stood upon and remains standing today. There is law to keep Judaism alive, the sound foundation of ceremonies and rituals.

VI

THE MOHEL

~~~~~~

Unites Skill with Culture

and Child with God

PAINLESS PROCEDURE
UNITING SKILL WITH CULTURE
MODERN MOHEL
TRUE SPECIALIST IN HIS FIELD
MODERN MEDICAL FACTS

As the First Rays of Sunshine
Illumine the Day so the
Mitzvah of Milah Guarantees
a Bright Future for the Young
Lad as He Takes His Place as
a Member of the Jewish Fold

Unites Skill with Culture . . .

PAINLESS PROCEDURE

THE technique of the modern mohel combines spiritual and surgical skill. The expert mohel is a specialist who has advanced this procedure to the most modern medical standards.

The mohel who is fully conversant with all medical techniques performs an almost bloodless and painless circumcision. The wound heals uneventfully in a short period of time, causing no concern to baby and parents.

We must turn to modern science if we are interested in justifying the possible halakhic (legalistic) reason for choice of the eighth day for performance of brit milah. The Torah gives us no clue other than the command, "He shall be circumcised on the eighth day." We know that in the normal newborn baby, the blood clotting factors do not fully come into play much before that time. During the earlier days, the prothrombin level, the substance necessary for blood clotting, is low, hence predisposes to free bleeding; on the eighth day the prothrombin level is more likely to be within normal limits.

All instruments in use for circumcision today were invented and perfected by those who practiced milah as a profession. The use of advanced instruments in the hands of a competent mohel avoids any danger of bleeding or infection.

The mohel, constantly progressing in skill and knowledge, has rendered circumcision an art of flawless perfection. Healing and post-operative care are completely successful, and recovery takes a short period. Twenty-four to forty-eight hours were required with the old technique.

A brit can be performed at home without endangering the welfare of the child, because of the mohel's modern antiseptic technique. Seventy precent of circumcisions today are performed at home, for post-operative handling of the little patient does not necessitate hospital care.

The operation is as old as Judaism and as young as we keep it alive. The modern mohel combines safety with sentiment.

UNITING SKILL WITH CULTURE

The fact that a physician may be of the Jewish faith does not qualify him to circumcise according to the Bible— only to perform surgery. The mohel should be a pious individual; circumcision is not merely a surgical process, but a law and ritual commanded by the Bible.

When a physician who is not specially trained as a mohel performs this holy religious rite, the brit becomes not a brit but a surgical procedure. The prayers recited by a rabbi while the physician acts do not render this proper.

Jewish law and tradition state that the ritual circumcision is not a mere health measure. A brit milah is achieved only when the laws of our Torah are fulfilled. Can we have a physician? Only if he be a zealous pious Jew, learned in Jewish tradition and especially trained for this operation.

"He who omits the sign of the covenant destroys the

covenant itself" (GENESIS XVII:14). God's laws demand recognition of the ideas on which they are based.

These are the requirements:

Only the physical act of an expert mohel inspired by zeal for the Jewish religion renders a *brit milah* proper.

Therefore:

If an ordinary physician not trained as a mohel performs circumcision, even if a rabbi is present and reads the prayers, what results is not *milah,* but only an act of surgery.

So adept is the experienced mohel that even physicians prefer his services to that of a surgeon when circumcision is to be performed on their sons.

Through the mohel we thank God for the miracle of life, and dedicate the infant to a life of devotion to God.

THE MODERN MOHEL

The modern mohel is trained in Jewish tradition and operative techniques. The time-honored technique as practiced for four thousand years has in no way deteriorated, but only improved, and still remains in strict accordance with the ancient laws set down in the Torah.

He represents millenia of solid Jewish experience. It is a far cry from the days of Moses and Joshua when circumcision was performed with sharp stones. This generation has witnessed many radical changes in the technique of the timeless law in matters of securing maximum protection of the child, hygienic and medical.

The hospital patient is grateful to the hospital officials, administrator, nurse, and medical director or attending physician, who have had the foresight to select a competent and experienced mohel.

TRUE SPECIALIST IN HIS FIELD

Jewish law has prescribed a series of stringent requirements for licensing a mohel. Not only must he have expert surgical skill acquired through training and experience, but be a man of learning and zeal for Jewish tradition. He has received a certificate of his qualifications.

In the time of the Talmud specially qualified surgeons were appointed for this operation. In fact, a Circumcision Street, where professional mohalim lived, is mentioned in the Talmud. At the present time, it is done by laymen, who must receive training in asepsis and technique at the hands of a doctor appointed by the ecclesiastical authorities. This rite can be performed only by an observant Jew.

Circumcision is now practiced universally. Such is the skill of the experienced mohel that Queen Elizabeth II of England, upon the birth of Crown Prince Charles, retained the services of Dr. Jacob Snowman, official mohel of the London Jewish community, for this delicate task.

MODERN MEDICAL FACTS

A mohel performs circumcision every day of the year; and because of this special experience his knowledge of medical and surgical facts concerning circumcision is complete and authoritative. Therefore, circumcision on the eighth day (dictated by the Bible) is accepted by many authorities as advantageous physically as well as spiritually.

A further vindication of Jewish tradition is that separation of the mucous membrane from the glans (a necessary procedure) is much more difficult before the eighth day, because it is only on or after that day that the adhesions cease to cling.

Another fact accepted by modern medical science is that newborn infants' blood clotting factors are properly functioning on the eighth day.

The dictates of the Bible are vindicated as it is noted that only in rare instances have children died after this rite because of loss of blood. The talmudists, some two thousand years ago, observed that some women, themselves immune,

transmit to their sons a rare affliction we now call hemo-
philia, which can cause death through bleeding of any
wound. They therefore made a rule that where parents have
lost a child due to loss of blood in circumcision, they were
forbidden to perform this rite for any sons born thereafter.

It is also interesting to note that in research on cancer
of the penis not one known case has been found on a Jew
circumcised at the beginning of his life. Neither the Jewish
male nor female has immunity to epidermoid cancer in
other sections of the body, but women married to circumcised men are not prone to cancer of the cervix. Therefore
this is not a racial immunity; medical literature mentions
Jewish men who are uncircumcised developing penis cancer (which constitutes about 3% of all cancer in men). This
clearly demonstrates that circumcision makes it possible to
stunt or stop altogether accumulation of smegma, the secre-
tion that collects beneath the uncircumcised foreskin.

Although we are proud of our proved theories concerning the rite, we must never forget that brit milah is intended as a *spiritual rather than physical act*. God's laws
demand the basic concept of a divine act spiritually fulfilling
the commandment as prescribed.

1. It is a sign of the covenant between God and the
   Jews.
2. It reminds Jews to maintain good health and be
   alert to hygienic demands.
3. It turns out to be sound hygiene and prevents trans-
   mission of disease.
4. It reminds man to perfect himself.

Informed people everywhere are now being circumcised.

The Jews have followed Mosaic law with a confidence
which modern medicine progressively ratifies. The medical
endorsement is not, however, the glory of Judaism. It is a
footnote. It is always important to remember that Jews
circumcise their sons basically for religious purposes.

VII

PRAYERS

‿‿

And God Blessed Them . . .

MOTHER'S PRAYER
FATHER'S PRAYER
GRANDPARENT'S PRAYER
GODPARENT'S PRAYER
SANDEK'S PRAYER

And God Blessed Them and
said, Be Fruitful and Multiply
and Fill the Earth

GENESIS I:28

And God Blessed Them . . .

We Find Strength in Prayer, Faith and Love in

Addressing God, Therefore the Following

Prayers Are Suggested

— Before the Brit —

MOTHER'S PRAYER
(As the baby is brought to the mohel)

BLESSED art Thou, O Lord our God, King of the universe, who hast blessed our union with Thy great gift of life. I thank Thee, O Lord our God, for leading me through anxiety and fear and bestowing this light to replace the uncertainty. Thy great power was with me and my spirit was uplifted and exalted in Thy creation. Thy miracle of love is in the mystery of life coming into being. We thank Thee for the miracle of human experience in the birth of our child. Mayest Thou grant us—mother, father, and child—strength in mind and spirit to raise this infant that he may become the pride and joy of our hearts and be of great honor to God and man.

AMEN

103

FATHER'S PRAYER

O Lord, Almighty God, I stand today in Thy presence, eager to re-enact a duty which is accepted by me with joy and obeyed with sincerity.

Circumcision is of such importance that heaven and earth are maintained only by fulfillment of Thy covenant.

I give my newborn son into the hands of the mohel, whom I charge with the duty of circumcision in accordance with Thy law.

My son, who is eight days old, will on this day be brought into the holy covenant of our father Abraham.

May it be Thy will, O Lord our God, to assure my precious son a future unto Thee, that he grow and live to be a credit to Thee, O God, to country and to people.

AMEN

GRANDPARENT'S PRAYERS

Almighty God! Blessed be the hour that I again open my heart unto my Deliverer to adore and glorify Thy name, for Thy divine wisdom and kindness.

Today we celebrate the coming into Israel of a new son. This ritual of our forefathers is a symbol of a covenant entered into with Thee to bless Thy holy name.

Thou, O Lord, in Thy mercy gavest to my grandchild, a being now helpless, the capability in time to achieve greatness upon this earth.

May it please Thee to bless my child's house with health, happiness, and contentment, so that all the members of my family be able to serve Thee in joy.

Bless Thee, heavenly Father, hear my voice. May the child grow in vigor of mind to become a ben Torah, a true bar mitzvah, an intelligent and informed human being; and may he happily attain the marriage canopy and a life of good deeds. Bless our children, that they may become the pride and joy of our hearts, and find favor in the eyes of God and man.

AMEN

GODPARENT'S PRAYERS

May the Father of compassion and truth have mercy upon this child He lovingly tended, and upon all who gather here today to remember the covenant with the patriarchs. Thou hast graciously granted us this hour of honor and pride as we spread our loving arms to embrace our little ward. Lord, may the mother of today and the father whom we release for the hour find this an acceptable day to the Lord. Thou hast brought us the joy foretold by Elijah in keeping Thy covenant.

AMEN

SANDEK'S PRAYER

Blessed art Thou, O Lord our God, King of the universe, who hast commanded that Thy will be done. Behold, I come to be sandek at this brit milah, and I shall be the throne and altar upon which the circumcision is performed. May it be Thy will, O Lord our God and God of our fathers, that this altar be as an atonement and a symbol of our allegiance to this holy covenant.

May this brit be completed with the intent for which it was designed, and may the circumcision be considered as important and holy as the incense used in Thy holy Temple. May we fulfill the Torah verse which says: "An eight day old child shall be circumcised." As representative of the mother of this child and in loyalty to Elijah, I declare the ritual in accordance with Thy will. Bless the Lord, His substance, and accept the work of His hands. And let the graciousness of the Lord our God be upon us.

Establish Thou also upon us the work of our hands, yea, the work of our hands establish Thou it. What can I render unto the Lord for all His benefits towards me? I will offer to Thee the sacrifice of thanksgiving, and will call upon the name of the Lord. I will say my vows unto the Lord, yea, in the presence of all His people; in the courts of the Lord's house, in the midst of Thee, O Jerusalem. Praise ye the Lord.

AMEN

VIII

NAMES

~~~~~~

A Good Name is Rather To Be Chosen
Than Great Riches

PROVERBS XXII:1

THE CUSTOM OF NAMES
NAMING A NEWBORN DAUGHTER
SUGGESTED NAMES
GLOSSARY

Every Man Has Three Names:
One His Father and Mother Gave Him,
One Others Call Him,
And One He Acquires Himself.

ECCLESIASTES RABBAH 7:1.3

VIII

A Good Name is Rather to be Chosen . . .

There are no religious rules or regulations concerning the naming of a Jewish child. Contrary to public opinion, *there is no law on names,* only custom. Who names the baby in Jewish families is a matter of custom and sentiment rather than actual legislation.

The child may be named after any person—friend or relative—who is deceased. On the other hand, the infant need not be given the name of any particular person. Jewish children have been named after some famous tzaddik (rabbi), biblical characters, or noted people.

What should be kept in mind? It should be a Hebrew name selected from the rich and meaningful store in the sacred literature and history of our people (approximately 3,000 names are contained in the Bible).

The name given the newborn infant always has some meaning. To call a boy David is to associate the child with love. For David was called "beloved," Solomon the "wise king," and Abraham the "patriarch." A girl is called Ruth in anticipation that she will live up to the loyalty and devotion of the biblical Ruth.

Names translated into English have no necessary connection with Hebrew names. The Heberw is the way to carry on Jewish tradition. The child *must have a Hebrew name.*

Theoretically naming of the infant is the father's decision. If there is a choice between the name of the father's father and that of the mother's father, the paternal grandfather usually has preference. However, in some countries it is the mother's privilege to name the firstborn child.

It is permissible to convert a name by translating from the feminine to the masculine (Chayah to Chayim). By the same token the name Chayah can be used at a future date for the baby's sister. The Jewish name does not have to correspond with the English.

Throughout the ages, every Jew has felt the desire to have his name remembered and firmly fixed in the living chain.

Naming of a child is intended to keep alive family memories. A boy who carries through life the name of a grandfather is a living reminder and constant memorial of the grandfather.

The Ashkenazim (from Central and Eastern Europe) are accustomed to commemorate their beloved ancestors by naming a child after a deceased loved one.

The reason for divergent practices among Jewish people of various countries may be associated with the folklore of the time. Ashkenazi Jews identified the name with the soul more closely than did the Sephardim. Ashkenazim felt it disastrous to name the child after any person, living or dead, for fear that it would rob the living of his full life and would disturb the spirit of the dead. Even though the rabbis recognized this fear as based on superstition, they made no attempt to discourage the custom, since it had some practical value. For when two members of the family bear the same name it can lead to confusion.

At present we are left with two customs (which are not actually written law but in the minds of most Jews is as binding as law). With Jews who follow Central and East European tradition, children are usually named after a deceased relative whose memory the parents wish to honor. Among the Sephardim (from Middle Eastern countries) a son is usually named after his living grandfather.

There were many reasons, to encourage memorializing the name of an honored grandparent, uncle, or aunt, whose qualities the parents would like to see reborn in their child. In either tradition similar given names remain in the family for generations.

Because of the widespread dispersion of Jews in many lands, the habit of using non-Jewish first names translated from the Hebrew name of a deceased relative, has come into general practice. In America and many European countries, a child is often given both a Hebrew name after a relative and one common to the land of his birth.

Today in Israel children have names linked with events, as well as with personalities in Jewish history. Israel can now claim charming Hebrew names rich in association and symbolic of kinship with their people.

There is a saying in the Mishnah, "The crown of a good name excels all other crowns, including the crown of learning, of priesthood, and even of royalty." Jewish history reveals the importance of Jewish names in our people's survival. "A good name is better than precious oil" (PROVERBS XXII:I). While the Mishnah refers to a man's reputation, it was believed that a person's name was associated with his character.

"Man has three names: one by which his parents call him; another, by which he is known to the outside world; and a third, the most important of all, the name which his own deeds have procured for him" (TANCHUMA VAYYAKEL).

Neither law nor tradition dictates the form and manner of naming the Jewish child. Jewish law opposes the superstitious belief that physical harm will come to a child named

after a young departed member or after a living person in
the family.

ויקרא שמה בישראל

NAMING A NEWBORN DAUGHTER

The ritual for naming a Jewish girl takes place during
a synagogue service.

The father, or a close member of the family, should
attend worship as soon as possible after the girl is born. It
should be a service at which the Torah is read: Sabbath
morning or afternoon, Monday or Thursday morning, or a
new moon morning, any holyday, or any time specially provided. The father gives thanks and is called up to the Torah
to proclaim his daughter's Hebrew name.

Among orthodox and conservative Jews the father is
honored with an aliyah, and God's blessing is invoked for his
new daughter and the mother's recovery. In Reform temples
the naming service is often delayed until the mother and
father attend together on a Friday night or Sabbath morning.

Among Ashkenazic Jews a baby girl is named on the
first Sabbath. In many countries, the child is brought before
the altar of the synagogue to be blessed by the rabbi.

Before the father attends his synagogue for that purpose, he should know the following: his own Jewish name
and the name of his father; his descent, kohen, Levi, or
Yisrael; his wife's Jewish name and her mother's name:
the Jewish name to be bestowed on the infant.

When the father attends the service, and is given an
aliyah, he is expected to recite the following prayers.

בָּרְכוּ אֶת־יְיָ הַמְבֹרָךְ.

BOR-KHU ES ADO-NOY HA-ME-VO-RAKH
"Bless ye the Lord who is to be blessed"

(*Congregation*)

בָּרוּךְ יְיָ הַמְבֹרָךְ לְעוֹלָם וָעֶד

BA-RUKH ADO-NOY HA-ME-VO-RAKH LE-O-LAM
VA-ED

"Blessed is the Lord, who is to be blessed forever and ever."
(The above is repeated by the recipient of the aliyah.)

בָּרוּךְ אַתָּה יְיָ, אֱלֹהֵינוּ מֶלֶךְ הָעוֹלָם, אֲשֶׁר בָּחַר בָּנוּ מִכָּל
הָעַמִּים וְנָתַן לָנוּ אֶת תּוֹרָתוֹ. בָּרוּךְ אַתָּה יְיָ, נוֹתֵן הַתּוֹרָה.

BA-RUKH A-TAH ADO-NOY ELO-HEY-NU ME-LEKH
HA-O-LAM A-SHER BA-HAR BA-NU MI-KAL HA-A-
MIM VE-NA-SAN LA-NU ES-TO-RA-SO. BA-RUKH A-
TAH ADO-NOY NO-SEIN HA-TO-RAH.

"Blessed art Thou, O Lord our God, King of the universe,
who hast chosen us from among all peoples, and hast given
us Thy Torah. Blessed art Thou, O Lord, who givest the
Torah."

After the reading, the following blessing is said:

בָּרוּךְ אַתָּה יְיָ, אֱלֹהֵינוּ מֶלֶךְ הָעוֹלָם, אֲשֶׁר נָתַן לָנוּ תּוֹרַת אֱמֶת
וְחַיֵּי עוֹלָם נָטַע בְּתוֹכֵנוּ. בָּרוּךְ אַתָּה יְיָ, נוֹתֵן הַתּוֹרָה.

BA-RUKH A-TAH ADO-NOY ELO-HEY-NU ME-LEKH
HA-O-LAM A-SHER NA-SAN LA-NU TO-RAS E-MES
VE-ḤA-YEY O-LAM NA-TA BE-SO-KHEY-NU. BA-RUKH
A-TAH ADO-NOY NO-SEIN HA-TO-RAH.

"Blessed art Thou, O Lord our God, King of the universe,
who hast given us the Torah of truth, and hast planted
everlasting life in our midst. Blessed art Thou, O Lord, who
givest the Torah."

The baby's Hebrew name is then publicly announced in a prayer by the rabbi or cantor, and a special prayer for the health and welfare of the mother and the newborn daughter.

In many congregations a certificate is issued by the synagogue office, on which the child's name and birth date and place of the ceremony are recorded.

MAZAL TOV!   מזל טוב!

ויקרא שמה בישראל

Certificate of the Newly Born Daughter

THIS IS TO CERTIFY THAT

_____

daughter of

English	Name of father (*) ·	Hebrew

English	Name of mother	Hebrew

English	Date of birth	Hebrew

The Name Bestowed Upon Her for Honor, Pride, and Glory is

_____

Hebrew name

On the_____day of the Hebrew month of_____

in the year 57____

MAY SHE BE A BLESSING TO HER PARENTS, RELATIVES, TO ISRAEL AND TO MANKIND.

At_____In_____

Congregation   Address   City   State

_____   _____

Obstetrician   Rabbi or Cantor

(*) Kohen ☐ Levi ☐

HEBREW AND JEWISH MALE NAMES
(alphabetically in English)
an asterisk (*) denotes a Jewish name
(df) means *derived from*

A

Aaron, Aharon – Teaching; mountaineer	אַהֲרֹן
Abba – Father	אַבָּא
Achiezer, Ahiezer – Brother, helper	אֲחִיעֶזֶר
Adam – Earth	אָדָם
Adoniyah, Adonijah – God is my Lord	אֲדֹנִיָה
Akiva, Akiba – Supplanter	עֲקִיבָא
Alexander – Defender of men	אֲלֶכְסַנְדֶּר
Alon – Oak	אָלוֹן
*Alter – Old one; other one	*אַלטֶער
Amatz, Amaziah – Strong, Courageous,	אָמוֹץ, אֲמַצְיָה
Amichai – My folk is alive	עֲמִיחַי
Ami-el – Of the family of God	עֲמִיאֵל
Amikam – Nation arisen	עֲמִיקָם
Aminadav, Aminadab – Kin of the prince	עֲמִינָדָב
Amir – Proclaimed	אָמִיר
Amiram – Lofty people	עֲמִירָם
Ammitai – Truthful	אֲמִיתַּי
Amnon – Faithful	אַמְנוֹן
Amos – Burdened	עָמוֹס

Amram – Mighty nation	עַמְרָם
*Anshel, Anshil – (df) Asher	*אַנשֶׁעל, אַנשִׁיל (אָשֵׁר)
Ari – Lion	אֲרִי
Ariel – Lion of God	אֲרִיאֵל
Arnon – Roaring stream	אַרְנוֹן
Aron – Ark	אָרוֹן
Arye, Aryeh (*Leib)	אַרְיֵה, (לֵייבּ*)
Asher – Blessed; happy	אָשֵׁר
Avadya, Obadiah – Servant of God	עֲבַדְיָה
Aviad – Father forever	אֲבִיעַד
Avichai – My father alive	אֲבִיחַי
Aviezer, Abiezer – Father helper	אֲבִיעֶזֶר
Avigdor – Father protector	אֲבִיגְדוֹר
Avimelech, Abimelech – Father king	אֲבִימֶלֶךְ
Avinadov, Abinadab – Generous father	אֲבִינָדָב
Avinoam, Abinoam – Pleasant father	אֲבִינֹעַם
Aviram, Abiram – Father of heights	אֲבִירָם
Avner, Abner – Father of light	אַבְנֵר
Avraham, Abraham – Father of multitude	אַבְרָהָם
Avram, Abram – Father of elevation	אַבְרָם
Avshalom, Absalom – Father of peace	אַבְשָׁלוֹם
Azaryah, Azaryahu – God helps	עֲזַרְיָה, עֲזַרְיָהוּ
Azi – Strong	עַזִי
Azri-el – Help of God	עַזְרִיאֵל

B

Barak – Lightning	בָּרָק
Baruch – Blessed	בָּרוּךְ
*Bendit (Baruch)	*בֶּענדִיט (בָּרוּךְ)
*Beinish – (df) Benjamin	*בֵּיינִיש, בֵּינָש (בִּנְיָמִין)
Ben-Ami – Son of my people	בֶּן־עַמִּי
Ben-Tziyon, Ben-Zion – Son of Zion	בֶּן־צִיּוֹן
*Ber, Baer (Dov)	*בֶּער (דוֹב)
*Berel, Beril (Dov)	*בֶּערְעל, בֶּעריל (דוֹב)
*Berish (Issachar Dov) – Precious	*בֶּעריש (יְשָׂכָר דוֹב)
Betzalel, Bezalel – In the shadow of God	בְּצַלְאֵל
Binah – Understanding; wisdom	בִּינָה
Binyamin, Benjamin – Son of right hand	בִּנְיָמִין, בִּנְיָמָן
Boaz – Fleetness	בֹּעַז, בּוֹעַז
*Bontche, Bonche – (df) Binyamin	*בָּאנטשֶׁע (בִּנְיָמִין)
*Buna – (df) Binyamin	*בּוּנָא (בִּנְיָמִין)
*Bunim – (df) Binyamin	*בּוּנִים (בִּנְיָמִין)
*Bunin – (df) Binyamin	*בּוּנִין (בִּנְיָמִין)

C

Caleb – Dog	כָּלֵב
Carmel – Garden	כַּרְמֶל
Carmi – Vine dresser	כַּרְמִי
Chafni, Chafnoi – Fighter; pugilist	חָפְנִי, חָפְנָי
*Chana, Hannah (Elchanan)	*חָנָא (אֶלְחָנָן)
Chamiyah, Hamiyah – God's warmth	חַמִיָה

Chananeil – God is gracious	חֲנַנְאֵל
Chananya, Chananyahu, Hananiah God is gracious	חֲנַנְיָה, חֲנַנְיָהוּ
Chanina, Chanani – (df) Chanah	חֲנִינָא, חֲנַנִי
Chanoch – Initiating	חֲנוֹךְ
Chanun, Hanun – Gracious	חָנָן
Chasdai, Hasdai – Righteous	חַסְדָּאִי
*Chatzkel – (df) Chizkiya	*חַאצְקֶעל (חִזְקִיָה)
Chavakuk, Habakkuk – Embrace	חֲבַקּוּק
Chavivi, Chaviv, Habib – Beloved	חֲבִיבִי, חָבִיב
Chayim, Hayim – Life	חַיִּים
*Chazkel – (df) Chizkiya	*חַזְקֶאל (חִזְקִיָה)
Chizkiya, Chizkiyahu, Hezekiah Might of God	חִזְקִיָה, חִזְקִיָהוּ
Chilkiya, Hilkiah – God's portion	חִלְקִיָה
Chiram, Hiram – Freeborn; noble	חִירָם
Chisda – Zealous	חִסְדָּא
Chur, Hur – Pit	חוּר

D

Dan – Judge	דָּן
Daniyel, Daniel – God's judge	דָּנִיאֵל
David – Beloved	דָּוִד
Doron – Gift	דּוֹרוֹן
Doson, Dathan – Gift	דָּתָן
Dov (*Ber) – Bear	דּוֹב (*בֶּער)

E

Ehud – Biblical name   אֵהוּד

Eliezer, Eleazar – God aids   אֶלְעָזָר ,אֱלִיעֶזֶר ,אֶלְעָזֶר

Efrayim, Ephraim – Fruitful   אֶפְרַיִם

Elchanan, Elkan – God is gracious   אֶלְחָנָן

Elimelech – God is king   אֱלִימֶלֶךְ

Elisha – God is salvation   אֱלִישָׁע

Eliyahu, Elijah – The Lord is God   אֵלִיָּהוּ ,אֵלִיָּה

Elkanah – God possessed   אֶלְקָנָה

Elyakim, Eliakim – God established   אֶלְיָקִים

Elye, Ellie – (df) Eliyahu   עֶלִי ,עֶלְיֶע

Ethan – Strong   אֵיתָן

Ezer, Ezra – Help   עֶזְרָא ,עֵזֶר

F

Feitel (Chayim)   (חַיִּים) פֵייטֶעל

Feivel – (df) Eliezer   (אֱלִיעֶזֶר) פַייוֶועל

Feibush, Feivish – (df) Eliezer   (אֱלִיעֶזֶר) פֵייבוּשׁ, פַייוִוישׁ

Fishel – (df) Ephraim   (אֶפְרַיִם) פִישֶׁעל, פִישֶׁל

G

Gad – Good fortune   גָּד

Gadil – (df) Gad   (גָּד) גָּאדִיל

Gadol – Large   גָּדוֹל

Gavriel, Gabriel – God is my strength   גַּבְרִיאֵל

Gedalya, Gedaliah, Gedalyahu – God   גְּדַלְיָהוּ ,גְּדַלְיָה
    has made great

Gedi – Cub   גְּדִי

Gershom – A stranger there   גֵּרְשָׁם

Gershon – Stranger there; expulsion   גֵּרְשׁן

Getzil, Getzel – (df) Elyakim   גֶּעטצִיל, גֶעצִיל (אֶלְיָקוּם)

Geyora – Shooter   גְּיוֹרָא

Gideon – Cutter down (Soldier)   גִּדְעוֹן

Gil – Happiness   גִיל

Gilon – Circle   גִילוֹן

Gimpel – (df) Mordecai   גִּימְפֶּעל (מָרְדְכַי)

Gronum – Throat   גְּרוֹנָם

Gurion – Young lion   גוּרִיוֹן

H

Hadar – Glory   הָדָר

Hagai – Meditation   הַגַאי

Henoch, Enoch (Chanoch) – Initiating (חֲנוֹךְ) הֶעֱנוּךְ, הֶעֱנַאךְ

Hersh, Hirsh (Tzvi)   הֶערְשׁ, הִירשׁ (צְבִי)

Hershel, Hirshel (Tzvi)   הֶערְשֶׁעל, הִירשֶׁעל (צְבִי)

Hertz, Herzel (df) Naftali   הֶערְץ, הֶערְצֶל (נַפְתָּלִי)

Heschel, Heshil (Tzvi)   הֶעשֶׁעל, הֶעשִׁיל (צְבִי)

Hillel – Praising; singing   הִלֵּל

Hosea – Salvation   הוֹשֵׁעַ

I

Iddel – "Little Jew" – (df) Yehudah   אִידֶעל (יְהוּדָה)

Immanu-el – God with us   עִמָּנוּאֵל

Ira – A guardian	עִירָא
Iseail, Ithiel – God is with me	אִיתִיאֵל
*Isser (Yisra-el) – (df) Israel	*אִיסֶער (יִשְׂרָאֵל)
*Itche (Yitzchok) – "Little Isaac"	*אִיטשֶׁע (יִצְחָק)
Ittamar – Island of palms	אִיתָמָר
Ittan, Ethan – Strength	אִיתַן, אֵיתָן
*Itzik (Yitzchak)	*אִיצִיק (יִצְחָק)
*Izik (Yitzchak)	*אַייזִיק (יִצְחָק)

K

Kalman – Merciful	קַלְמָן
Kalonymus – Merciful; (df) Kalman	קַלוֹנִימוּס (קַלְמָן)
Keren – Stalk	קֶרֶן
Kasri-el – God's crown	כַּתְרִיאֵל
Kidor – Generation	כִּידוֹר
*Kiva – (df) Akiva	*קִיבָא (עֲקִיבָא)
*Koppel – (df) Yaakov	*קָאפֶּעל (יַעֲקֹב)
Ko'resh, Cyrus – Sun	כּוֹרֶשׁ
Kusa – (df) Yekusiel; fear of God	קוּסָא

L

Laadan – For delight	לַעְדָּן
Lael – Belonging to God	לָאֵל
*Laib, Leb, Leibel (Aryeh)	*לֵייב, לֵיב, לֵייבֶּעל (אַרְיֵה)
*Laibush, Lebish (Aryeh)	*לֵייבּוּשׁ, לֵייבִּישׁ (אַרְיֵה)
Lapidos, Lapidoth – Torches	לַפִּידוֹת
Lavan, Laban – White	לָבָן

Layve, Levi – Joined	לֵוִי
*Layzer, Leizer (Eliezer)	*לֵייזֶר (אֱלִיעֶזֶר)
*Lemmel – Lamb	*לֶעמֶעל
Lemuel – Devoted to God	למוּאֵל
Lev, Leb – Heart	לֵב
*Lipman, Lippe – dim. of Eliezer	*לִיפְמַאן, לִיפֶּע (אֱלִיעֶזֶר)
*Litman – dim. of Eliezer	*לִיטמַאן (אֱלִיעֶזֶר)

M

Manuel – God reckons	מַנוּאֵל
*Manish – dim. of Menasseh	*מַאנִישׁ, מָאנִישׁ (מְנַשֶּׁה)
Mattisyahu, Mattos, Mattathias – Gift of God	מַתִּתְיָהוּ, מַטּוֹת
Matzliach – Successful	מַצלִיחַ
Mayir, Meir – Enlightener	מֵאִיר
Melech – King	מֶלֶךְ
Menachem (*Mendel) - Comforter	מְנַחֵם (מֶענדֶעל*)
Menachem (Nachum) – Comforter	מְנַחֵם (נַחוּם)
Menasheh, Menasseh – Who forgets	מְנַשֶּׁה
*Mendel (Menachem)	*מֶענדֶעל (מְנַחֵם)
Meshulam – Peaceful	מְשׁוּלָם
Micha, Micah – Who is like God	מִיכָה
Micha-el, Michel, Michael – Who is like God	מִיכָאֵל, מִיכֶעל
Miron – Name of holy place	מִירוֹן
Mordechai, Mordecai – Warrior	מָרְדְּכַי
Mosheh, Moses – Drawn out	משֶׁה
*Mottel, Mottya – (df) Mordecai	*מָאטֶעל, מָאטיֶע (מָרְדְּכַי)

N

Naaman – Pleasant	נַעֲמָן
Nachman – Cómforter	נַחְמָן
Nachum, Nahum – Comfort	נָחוּם
Nadav, Nadab – Giver	נָדָב
Naftaly, Naphtali – My strife	נַפְתָּלִי
Nassan, Nathan – Gift	נָתָן
*Nateh – He gave	*נָאטֶע
Nechemya, Nehemiah – God comforts	נְחֶמְיָה
Nesanel, Nathaniel – Gift of God	נְתַנְגְאֵל
Nesanyah, Nesanyahu, Nethaniah – God gave	נְתַנְיָה, נְתַנְיָהוּ
Nissan, Nisan – Month of flowers	נִיסָן
Nissim – Wonders; miracles	נִסִּים
Noach, Noah – Rest	נֹחַ
Noam – Pleasant	נֹעַם

O

Oded – Encourage	עוֹדֵד
Ophir – Biblical name	אוֹפִיר
Ovadiah, Obadiah – Servant of God	עוֹבַדְיָה
Oved, Obed – Worshiper; worker	עוֹבֵד
Ozer – Helper	עוֹזֵר

P

Palti, Palti-el – God liberates	פַּלְטִי, פַּלְטִיאֵל
Peretz, Perez – Breach	פֶּרֶץ

Pessach, Pesach – Spared   פֶּסַח

Pesachya, Pethahiah – God looses   פְּתַחְיָה, פְּסַחְיָא

Pinchos, Phineas – Mouth of brass;   פִּינְחָס, פִּנְחָס
  dark complexion

*Pinye – (df) Pinchos   *פִּינְיֶע (פִּנְחָס)

R

Raanan – Fresh; luxuriant   רַעֲנָן

Rachmiel – Whom God loves   רַחְמִיאֵל

Rechavia – Breadth   רְחַבְיָה

Re'uven, Reuben – Behold, a son   רְאוּבֵן

Rom – Height   רָם

Ron – Sing   רוֹן

Ronon – Singing   רוֹנֵן

R'phael, Raphael – God heals   רְפָאֵל

S

Saadya – God's helper   סַעַדְיָה

Sasson – Joy   שָׂשׂוֹן

*Sender – (df) Alexander   *סֶענְדֶער (אֲלֶכְּסַנְדֶר)

Shabsai, Sabbetai – Born on the Sabbath   שַׁבְּתַי

*Shachna – Close to God   *שַׁכְנָא

Shalom – Peace   שָׁלוֹם

Shammai – (df) Shemayahu   שַׁמַּאי

Sha-ul, Saul – Asked for   שָׁאוּל

Shevna, Shebna – Tender youth   שֶׁבְנָא

Shays, Seth – Garment; appointed   שֵׁת

Shelomo, Solomon – Peaceable   שְׁלֹמֹה

*Shepsil – (df) Shabsai   שֶׁעפּסִיל (שַׁבְּתַי)

Shevach – Praise   שֶׁבַח

Shim'on, Simeon, Simon – Hearing, with acceptance   שִׁמְעוֹן

Shimshon, Sampson – Like the sun   שִׁמְשׁוֹן

Shmarya, Shmaryahu – God watches   שְׁמַרְיָה, שְׁמַרְיָהוּ

Shmaiah, Shmayahu – God hears   שְׁמַעְיָה, שְׁמַעְיָהוּ

*Shmerel – (df) Shmarya   שְׁמֶערֶעל (שְׁמַרְיָה)

Shmuel, Samuel – God hears   שְׁמוּאֵל

*Shneur (Zalman)   שְׁנֶיאוּר (זַלְמָן)

Shoam – Onyx   שׁוֹאַם, שֹׁהַם

*Sho'el – Asker   שׁוֹאֵל

*Shraga – Phoebus; sun   שְׁרַגָא

Simcha – Joy   שִׂמְחָה

Sinai – Clay desert   סִינַי

*Sonye – Wise   סָאנְיֶע

T

Tanchum – Comfort   תַּנְחוּם

Tarphon – Gatherer of leaves   טַרפוֹן

*Tevel – (df) David   טֶעבֶעל (דָוִד)

*Todros – Gift; (df) Alexander   טוֹדרוּס (אֶלֶכְּסַנְדֶּר)

Tuvya, Tuvyahu, Tobiah – God's goodness   טוּבִיָה, טוֹבִיָהוּ

*Tzallel, Zallel – (df) Bezalel   צַלְאֵל (בְּצַלְאֵל)

Tzemach, Zemach – Sprout   צֶמַח

Tzefanyah, Tzefanyahu, Zephaniah –   צְפַנְיָה, צְפַנְיָהוּ
    Treasured by God

Tzidkiah, Tzidkiyahu, Zedekiah –   צִדְקִיָה, צִדְקִיָהוּ
    God's justice

Tzion, Zion – Sunny mountain   צִיּוֹן

Tzadok, Zadok – Just   צָדוֹק

Tzuriel, Zuriel – God is my rock   צוּרִיאֵל

Tzvi, Zevi (*Hirsh) – Deer   צְבִי (הִירש*)

U

Uri – My light   אוּרִי

Uriah – Light of God   אוּרִיָה

Uriel – Light of God   אוּרִיאֵל

Uzziel – Power of God   עוּזִיאֵל

V

Velvel (Z'ev)   וֶעלְוֶועל (זְאֵב)

Volf (Z'ev)   וָאלְף (זְאֵב)

Y

Yaakov, Jacob – Supplanter; held by the heel   יַעֲקֹב

Yagil – He will rejoice   יָגִיל

Yankel – (df) Yaakov   יַאנְקעל (יַעֲקֹב)

Yardane, Jordan – Descending   יַרְדֵן

Yashar, Jashar – Upright   יָשָׁר

Yechezkiel, Ezekiel – Might of God   יְחֶזְקָאל

Yechiel, Jehiel – God liveth   יְחִיאֵל

Yechizkiyahu – Might of God   יְחִזְקִיָהוּ

Yedidyah, Jedediah – Beloved of God   יְדִידְיָה

Yefes, Japhet – Handsome   יֶפֶת

Yehoash, Jehoash – God gave   יְהוֹאָשׁ, יוֹאָשׁ

Yehonadov, Nadab, Jonadab – God giveth   יְהוֹנָדָב, יוֹנָדָב

Yehonasan, Yonasan, Jonathan – Gift of God   יְהוֹנָתָן, יוֹנָתָן

Yehudah, Judah – Praised   יְהוּדָה

Yehudi – Jew   יְהוּדִי

Yehoshua, Joshua – God's help   יְהוֹשֻׁעַ

Yekusiel, Kusiel, Jekuthiel – Fear of God   יְקוּתִיאֵל, קוּתִיאֵל

Yerucham, Jeruham – Loved; finding mercy   יְרוּחָם

Yerachmiel, Jerahmeel – Whom God loves   יְרַחְמִיאֵל

Yesaniel, Yethaniel, Jethaniel – God giveth   יְתַנִיאֵל

Yeshaya, Yeshayahu, Isaiah – God lends   יְשַׁעְיָה, יְשַׁעְיָהוּ

Yeshurun, Jeshurun – The right way   יְשֻׁרוּן

Yiftoch, Jephthah – Will open   יִפְתָּח

Yigal, Yigol – He will redeem   יִגְאַל, יִגְאָל

Yirmiya, Yirmiyahu, Jeremiah – God   יִרְמִיָה, יִרְמִיָהוּ
appointed.

Yishai, Jesse – Wealthy, gift   יִשַׁי

Yisrael, Israel – Prince of God; strove with God   יִשְׂרָאֵל

Yissachar, Issachar – There is a reward   יִשָׂשכָר, יִשָׂכָר

Yitzchak, Isaac – Sporting; will laugh   יִצְחָק

Yoav, Joab – Biblical name   יוֹאָב

Yochanan, Johanan – Grace of God   יוֹחָנָן

Yo-el, Joel – God prevails   יוֹאֵל

Yoir, Jair – He will enlighten   יָאִיר

Yomtov – Holiday   יום טוב

Yonah, Jonah – Dove   יוֹנָה

Yoram, Joram – High God   יוֹרָם

Yoron – Singing   יָרוֹן

Yosef, Joseph – God will increase   יוֹסֵף

Yoshiyah, Yoshiyahu, Josiah – God's help   יֹאשִׁיָה, יֹאשִׁיָהוּ

Yossel – (df) Yosef   יָאסֶעל (יוֹסֵף)

Yovin, Jabin – He will understand   יָבִין

Yudel – (df) Yehudah   יוּדֶעל (יְהוּדָה)

Z

Zaide – Elder   זֵיידֶע

Zalman – (df) Shelomo   זַלמָן (שְׁלֹמֹה)

Zangvil (Z'ev) – (df) Wolf   זַאנגוויל (זְאֵב)

Zanvil, Zanvill – (df) Shmuel   זַאנוויל (שְׁמוּאֵל)

Zavel (Z'ev) – (df) Wolf   זַאװֶעל (זְאֵב)

Zevudah – Gift   זְבוּדָה

Zevul, Zebul – Residence   זְבוּל

Zecharya, Zecharyahu, Zechariah – God remembers   זְכַרְיָה, זְכַרְיָהוּ

Zecher – Memory   זֵכֶר

Zelig, Zelik – Blessed   זֶעלִיג, זֶעלִיק

Zerachya, Zerachyahu, Zerahiah – God shines   זְרַחְיָה, זְרַחְיָהוּ

Zerubavel, Zerubbabel – Born at Babylon זְרוּבָּבֶל

Z'ev, Ze'ev – Wolf זְאֵב (וָואלף*)

Zevulun, Zebulun – Habitation זְבוּלוּן

Zimra – Song זִמְרָא

*Zindel, Zindil, Zundel – זִינדֶעל, זִינדִיל, זוּנדֶעל
  (df) Alexander (אַלֶכְּסַנְדֶּר)

Ziskind – (df) Alexander; "suess kind" זִיסקִינד (אַלֶכְּסַנְדֶּר)

Zissa – (df) Eliezer (perhaps from זִיסָא, זִיסיָא (אֱלִיעֶזֶר)
  German Suess)

Zissel – (df) Alexander זִיסֶעל (אַלֶכְּסַנְדֶּר)

Zohar – Light זֹהַר

Zarach, Zerach – Light rising זָרַח, זֶרַח

Zussha, Zusshe – (df) Eliezer זוּשָא, זוּשֶׁע (אֱלִיעֶזֶר)

Zussman – (df) Eliezer זוּזמַאן, זוּסמַאן (אֱלִיעֶזֶר)

HEBREW AND JEWISH FEMALE NAMES
(alphabetically in English)
an asterisk (*) denotes a Jewish name
(df) means *derived from*

A

Adah, Ada – Ornament	עָדָה
Adina – Slender, pliant	עֲדִינָה
Ahava, Ahuva – Love, Beloved	אַהֲבָה, אֲהוּבָה
*Aidel – Delicate (German)	*אײדֶעל
Alexandra – (df) Alexander; defender of men	אַלֶכְּסַנְדְרָה
Alizah – Joyous	עֲלִיזָה
*Alte – Old one	*אַלְטֶע
•Amira – Ear of grain	עֲמִירָה
Arnonah – (df) Arnon; roaring stream	אַרְנוֹנָה
Asalyahu, Athalia – God is exalted	עֲתַלְיָה
Asna, Isna, Usna – Granary	אָסְנֶה אָסְנָא, אוּסְנָא
Atara, Atarah – Crown	עֲטָרָה
Avichayil, Abichail – Strong father	אֲבִיחַיִל
Avigail, Abigail – Father's joy	אֲבִיגַיִל
Aviva – Ear of corn, hence Spring	אֲבִיבָה
Aya – Bird	אַיָה
Ayalah – Hind, Roe	אַיָלָא

B

*Basha – (df) Bas-sheva	*בַּאשֶׁע (בַּת שֶׁבַע)
Bas-sheva, Bathsheba – Daughter of an oath	בַּת שֶׁבַע
*Basya – (df) Bas-sheva	*בַּאסִיע (בַּת שֶׁבַע)

Batya, Bitya – Daughter of God   בַּתְיָה, בִּתְיָה

Bas-Tzion, Bath-Zion – Daughter of Zion   בַּת צִיוֹן

Bayleh, Beileh – (df) Bas-sheva   בֵּיילֶע (בַּת שֶׁבַע)

Beruriah – Chosen by God   בְּרוּרִיָה

Binnah – Understanding   בִּינָה

Blima, Blime – Flower   בְּלִימַא, בְּלִימֶע

Bluma, Blume – Flower   בְּלוּמַא, בְּלוּמֶע

Breindel, Breine –   בְּרֵיינְדֶל, בְּרַיינדעל,

    (df) Brachah   בְּרֵיינֶע (בְּרָכָה)

Brachah – Blessing   בְּרָכָה

C

Carmela – Garden   כַּרְמֶלָה

Chamudah – Precious gift   חֲמוּדָה

Chanah, Hannah – Grace   חַנָה

Chasiyah – To find shelter   חֲסִיָה

Chasya, Chasye – (df) Chaya   חַסְיַא, חַסְיֶע, כַאסְיֶע (חַיָה)

Chantshe – (df) Chanah   חַאנטשֶׁע (חַנָה)

Chasidah – Pious woman   חֲסִידָה

Chavah, Eva – Life   חַוָה

Chaviva, Habibah – Beloved   חֲבִיבָה

Chaya – Life   חַיָה

Chayka – (df) Chaya   חַייקֶע (חַיָה)

Chedva – Joy   חֶדְוָה

Chephzivah, Hepzibah – My delight is in her   חֶפְצִיבָה

Chermona – Dedicated	חֶרְמוֹנָה
Chila – Strong	חִילָה
*Chine – (df) Chanah	*חִינֶע (חַנָה)
Chuldah, Hulda – World	חֻלְדָה
*Clara – Clean	*קְלֹאַרֹא, קְלַרֹה
Cochava – Star	כּוֹכָבָא

D

Dalith – Vine	דָלִית
Daliyah, Daliah – A branch	דָלִיָה
Daphne – Laurel	דַפְנָה
Davida – (df) David; Beloved	דָוִידָה
Derora – Freedom	דְרוֹרָה
Devorah, Deborah – Bee	דְבוֹרָה
Dinah – Adjudged, Vindicated	דִינָה
Ditza – Rejoicing	דִיצָה
Divsha – Honey	דִבְשָׁה
*Dobeh, Dobra – (df) Devorah	*דָאבֶּע, דָאבְּרֶע (דְבוֹרָה)
*Dobrush – (df) Devorah	*דָאברוּשׁ (דְבוֹרָה)
Dorith – Of this generation	דוֹרִית
*Doshke – (df) Devorah	*דָאשְׁקֶע (דְבוֹרָה)
*Dreizil – (df) Devorah	*דְרֵייזִיל (דְבוֹרָה)
*Droshe – (df) Devorah	*דְרָאשֶׁע (דְבוֹרָה)
Dura – Mother of pearl	דוּרָה (דְבוֹרָה)
*Dushe – (df) Devorah	*דוּשֶׁע (דְבוֹרָה)
*Dvashe – (df) Devorah	*דְוָואשֶׁע, דְבָאשֶׁע (דְבוֹרָה)

E

Edna – Pleasure	עֶדְנָה
*Elka, Elke – (df) Ellisheva	*אֶלְקָא, עֶלְקֶע
Ella – (df) Ellisheva	אֶלָּא, אֶלָּה (אֱלִישֶׁבַע)
Ellisheva, Elizabeth – Swear by God	אֱלִישֶׁבַע
Emunah – Faith	אֱמוּנָה
*Enye – (df) Chanah	*עֶנְיֶע
Ephrima – (df) Ephraim; Fruitful	אֶפְרִימָה
Erelah – Messenger, angel	אֶרְאֶלָה
Erith – Name of a flower	עִירִית
Esya, Ethiah – With God	אֶתְיָה
Ester, Esther – Star	אֶסְתֵּר
*Etta, Ette – (df) Orah	*עֶטָא, עֶטֶע (אוֹרָה)
*Ettel, Ethel – Noble	*עֶטֶעל

F

*Fayge, Feigel – (df) Tzipporah	*פֵייגֶע, פֵייגֶעל (צִפּוֹרָה)
*Frada, Frayde – (df) Simcha	*פְרַאדַא, פְרַיידֶע (שִׂמְחָה)
*Fradel, Fraydel – (df) Simcha	*פְרַאדֶעל, פְרַיידֶעל (שִׂמְחָה)
*Frieda – (df) Shalom – Peace	*פְרִידָה
*Fruma – Pious	*פְרוּמֶע
*Frumit – Pious	*פְרוּמִיט

G

Galilah – Name of a place in Israel	גָּלִילָה
Gavriella – (df) Gavriel; God is my strength	גַבְרִיאֶלָה

Gella, Gelle – Yellow | גֶעלַא, גֶעלֶע

Gene, Genye – of a garden | גֶענֶע, גֶענְיֶע

Geulah – Redemption | גְאוּלָה

Gevirah, Gevurah – Powerful ruler | גְבִירָה, גְבוּרָה

Gilah – Joy | גִילָה

Ginendel – (df) Chanah | גִינֶענדֶעל (חַנָה)

Gisha – (df) Chanah | גִישֶׁע (חַנָה)

Gitte, Gittel – (df) Tova | גִיטֶע, גִיטֶעל (טוֹבָה)

Glicka, Glicke – Happiness | גְלִיקַא, גְלִיקֶע

Golda, Goldie – (df) Zehava | גָאלדֶע (זֶהָבָה)

Guta, Gute – (df) Tova | גוּטַא, גוּטֶע (טוֹבָה)

H

Hadara – Splendor | הֲדָרָה

Hadassah – Myrtle | הֲדַסָה

Hentshe – (df) Chanah | הֶענטשֶׁע (חַנָה)

Henye – (df) Chanah | הֶענְיֶע (חַנָה)

Hessye – (df) Esther | הֶעסיֶע (אֶסתֵּר)

Hinde – (df) Chanah | הִינדֶע (חַנָה)

Hodel – Majesty | הָאדֶעל

Hodes – (df) Hadassah | הָאדֶעס (הֲדַסָה)

I

Iddel – Delicate (German) | אִידֶל

Ilana – Tree | אִילָנָה

Illat – (df) Ayala; Hind   אִילַת

*Inda, Inde – (df) Edna   אִינְדָא, אִינְדֶע (עֶדְנָה)

Iris – Name of a flower   אִירִיס

*Itta, Itte, Ittke – (df) Orah;   אִיטַא, אִיטֶע, אִיטקֶע (אוֹרָה)
    Light

K

*Kady, Kate – Pure (Greek)   *קֵיידִי

*Kayle – grey eyed   *קֵיילֶע

Kinneres, Kinneret – Harp   כִּנֶּרֶת

*Krayndel, Kreidel – (df) Atara; Crown   *קְרֵיינדֶעל (עֲטָרָה)

*Krona, Krone – (df) Atara   *קְרוֹינָא, קְרוֹינֶע (עֲטָרָה)

L

Laya, Leah – Wearied   לֵאָה

*Laytshe – (df) Laya   *לֵייטשֶׁע (לֵאָה)

Leila – Night   לַיְלָה

Levanah – Moon, White   לְבָנָה

*Libbe, Libbie – (df) Ahuvah   *לִיבֶּע, לִיבִּי (אֲהוּבָה)

Lily – Name of a flower   לִילִי

*Lipsha, Lipshe – (df) Ahuvah   *לִיפּשַׁא, לִיפּשֶׁע (אֲהוּבָה)

Liza – Joyous   לִיזָה

M

Malcah, Malkah – Queen   מַלְכָּה

Margalit – Pearl   מַרְגָּלִית

Mariasha, Mariashe – (df) מַארְיַאשָׁא, מַארְיַאשֶׁע (מִרְיָם)
 Miriam

Marninah – Causing to sing מַרְנִינָה

Marsa, Martha – Lady מָרְתָה

Masha – Brave מַאשֶׁע

Matanah – Gift מַתָּנָה

Mazal – Luck מַזָל

Meirah – (df) Meir; Enlightening מְאִירָה*

Menachemah – (df) Menahem; Consolation מְנַחֲמָה

Menuchah – Rest מְנוּחָה

Mesukah – Sweet מְתוּקָה

Michal – Small stream מִיכַל

Michla, Michle – Who is like God מִיכְלָא, מִיכְלֶע

Milcah – (df) Malcah מִילְכָּה

Minah – Of a kind מִינָה

Mindel – (df) Miriam מִינְדֶעל (מִרְיָם)

Minna, Minne – (df) Miriam מִינַא, מִינֶע (מִרְיָם)

Mintze, Mintza – (df) Miriam מִינְצַא, מִינְצֶע (מִרְיָם)

Mirel – (df) Miriam מִירֶעל (מִרְיָם)

Miriam – Sea of bitterness, contumacy מִרְיָם

Mirka, Mirke – (df) Miriam מִירְקַא, מִירְקֶע (מִרְיָם)

Mirtza, Mirtza – (df) Miriam מִירְצַא, מִירְצֶע (מִרְיָם)

Mattl, Mattel – (df) Mordecai; Brave מַאטְל, מַאטֶעל

N

Naamah – Pleasant	נַעֲמָה
Na'ana – Mint	נַעֲנָה
Naavah – Beautiful	נַאֲוָה
Na-ami, Naomi – Pleasant	נָעֳמִי
Nechama, Nehama – Comfort	נֶחָמָה
*Neche, Nechel – (df) Nechama	*נֶעכֶע, נֶעכֶעל (נֶחָמָה)
Nedivah – Generous	נְדִיבָה
Neorah – Light	נְאוֹרָה
*Neshe, Nessa – (df) Nissan; Month of flowers	*נֶעשֶׁע, נֶעסֶע
Nili – Israel's triumph shall not fail	נִילִי
Nira – Beam of loom	נִירָה
Nitzah – Sprout	נִיצָה
Nitzanah – Blossom	נִיצָנָה
Nitzchiyah – Everlasting	נִצְחִיָה
Noga – Shining	נוֹגַה
Nucha – Restful	נוּחָה
Nurith – Light	נוּרִית

O

Ophrah – Dust	עָפְרָה
Ora, Orah – Light	אוֹרָה
Ornah – Cedar	אוֹרְנָה

P

Peninah – Pearl	פְּנִינָה
Perachyah – Flowerful	פְּרַחְיָה
*Perril – (df) Peninah	*פֶּערִיל (פְּנִינָה)
*Pessa, Pessel, Pessye – (df) Peninah	*פֶּעסָע, פֶּעסֶעל, פֶּעסיֶע (פְּנִינָה)
*Pesha, Peshe – (df)Peninah	*פֶּעשָׁא, פֶּעשֶׁע (פְּנִינָה)
Poriah – Fruitful	פּוֹרִיָה
*Priva, Prive – (df) Peri; Fruit	*פְּרִינָא, פְּרִינֶוע

R

Raananah – (df) Raanan; fresh	רַעֲנָנָה
Rachama – Girl	רְחָמָה
Rachel – Ewe, Lamb	רָחֵל
*Rada, Rade – Rose	*רָאדַא, רָאדֶע
*Raisa, Raysel – (df) Shoshanah	*רֵייזֶע, רֵייזֶעל (שׁוֹשַׁנָה)
Rani, Ranit, Roni – Sing	רָנִי, רָנִית, רֹנִי
*Rashka, Rashke – (df) Rachel	*רַאשְׁקַא, רַאשְׁקֶע (רָחֵל)
*Rechell – (df) Rachel	*רֶעכֶעל (רָחֵל)
*Reicha – Rich	*רֵייכֶע
*Reina – Clean	*רֵיינֶע
Reiyah – Friendly	רְעֵיָה
Relle, Rellye – Garment	*רֶעלֶע, רֶעליֶע
Rena, Rina, Rinna, Rinnah – Song, joy	רְנָה
*Riva, Rive – (df) Rivka	*רִינָא, רִיבֶע (רִבְקָה)
Rivka, Rebecca – Bound	רִבְקָה

*Rose - (df) Shoshanah; Rose   ‫*רׂוֹיזֶע (שׁוֹשַׁנָה)‬

*Roza, Royze, Rosa – (df) Shoshanah   ‫רָאזַא, רָאזֶע (שׁוֹשַׁנָה)‬

Rus, Ruth -- Beauty, approval   ‫רוּת‬

S

Sa'adah – Help   ‫סַעֲדָה‬

Sarah – Princess   ‫שָׂרָה‬

Segulah – Precious   ‫סְגוּלָה‬

Semadar – Berry   ‫סְמָדָר‬

Shafrira – Pleasing   ‫שַׁפְרִירָה‬

*Shayndel, Shayne – (df) Yaffa   ‫*שֵׁיינְדֶעל, שֵׁיינֶע (יָפָה)‬

Sheva, Sheba – (df) Bas-sheva   ‫שֶׁבַע (בַּת שֶׁבַע)‬

Shifra – Beautiful   ‫שִׁפְרָה‬

*Shime – (df) Shimeon; Hearkening   ‫*שִׁימֶע‬

Shira – Song   ‫שִׁירָה‬

Shlomis, Shlomit – (df) Shelomo; Peace   ‫שְׁלוֹמִית‬

*Shosha – (df) Shoshanah   ‫*שָׁאשֶׁע (שׁוֹשַׁנָה)‬

Shoshanah – Rose   ‫שׁוֹשַׁנָה‬

*Shprintze – (df) Tikvah   ‫*שְׁפְּרִינצֶע (תִּקְוָה)‬

*Shterne - Star   ‫*שְׁטֶערנֶע‬

Shulamis, Shulamit – Peaceful   ‫שׁוּלַמִּית‬

*Silka – (df) Sarah   ‫*סִילקֶע (שָׂרָה)‬

*Silma -- Peace   ‫*סִילמַא‬

*Sima, Sime, Simca – Incense, treasure   ‫*סִימַא, סִימֶע, סִימקֶע‬

Simcha – Joy   שִׂמְחָה

*Sirka, Sirke – (df) Sarah   *סִירְקָא, סִירְקֶע (שָׂרָה)

*Slava, Slaveh – Splendor, elevated   *סְלאַוואַ, סְלאַוֶוע

*Sobel – Sustaining   *סוֹיבֶּעל

*Sosya, Sosye – (df) Sarah   *סאָסיאַ, סאָסיֶע (שָׂרָה)

T

Tamar, Tamara – Palm tree   תָּמָר, תָּמָרָה

*Tcharna, Tcherne – (df)   *טשאַרנאַ, טשאַרנֶע (אֲהוּבָה)
Ahuvah

Techiyah – Survival   תְּחִיָה

Tehillah – Praise   תְּהִלָה

*Tema, Teme – (df) Temima   *טֶעמאַ, טֶעמֶע (תְּמִימָה)

Temima – Perfect   תְּמִימָה

Tikvah – Hope   תִּקְוָה

*Tilleh, Tillie – Battlemaid; graceful tree   *טִילאַ, טִילֶע

Tirtzah, Tirzah – Pleasantness   תִּרְצָה

*Toba, Toibe – (df) Tova; Good, dove   *טוֹיבּאַ, טוֹיבֶּע (טוֹבָה)

*Toltza, Toltze – Sweet (Lat. dolcis)   *טאָלצאַ, טאָלצֶע

Tova – Good   טוֹבָה

*Trayndel, Trendel – (df) Emunah   *טְרײַנדֶעל (אֱמוּנָה)

Tzilla – Protection   צִילָה

*Tzippa – (df) Tzipporah   *צִיפֶּע (צִפּוֹרָה)

Tzipporah – Bird   צִפּוֹרָה

*Tziril, Tsirke, Cyril – (df) Sarah   צִירֶעל, צִירקֶע (שָׂרָה)

*Tzitel – (df) Zahava   צַייטֶעל (זְהָבָה)

Tzivia, Zibiah – (df) Tzvi; Deer   צְבִיָה, צְבִיָה

Tziyona – Zion   צִיוֹנָה

Tzophiah – Looking towards   צוֹפִיָה

V

Varda – Rose   וַרְדָה

Vardinah – Name of a flower   וַרְדִינָה

Vardith – Name of a flower   וַרְדִית

*Vichna, Vichne – (df) Chaya   וויכנַא, וויכנֶע (חַיָה)

*Vitel – (df) Chaya   וויטֶעל (חַיָה)

*Vitka, Vitke – (df) Chaya   וויטַקא, וויטקֶע (חַיָה)

Y

*Yacha, Yache – (df) Yocheved   יָאכַא, יָאכֶע (יוֹכֶבֶד)

*Yachna – (df) Yocheved   יַאכנֶע (יוֹכֶבֶד)

Yacoba, Jacoba – (df) Yakov; Supplanter   יַעֲקֹבָה

Ya-el, Jael – Mountain goat   יָעֵל

Yaffa, Jaffa – Beautiful   יָפָה

Yardenah – (df) River Jordan   יַרְדֵנָה

Yarkanah – Name of a bird 'Chloris'   יַרְקוֹנָה

Yedidah, Jedidah – Friend   יְדִידָה

Yehudis, Yehudit, Judith – (df) Yehudah; Praised יְהוּדִית

Yenta, Yente – Genteel יֶענטָא, יֶענטֶע

Yiskah, Iscah, Jessica – A covering יִסְכָּה

Yisraela, Israela – (df) Israel; Strove with God יִשְׂרָאֵלָה

Yitta, Yitte – (df) Ora יִטָא, יִטֶע (אוֹרָה)

Yocheved, Jochebed – Glory of God יוֹכֶבֶד

Yonah, Jonah – Dove יוֹנָה

Yoninah, Jonina – (df) Yonah; Little dove יוֹנִינָה

Yosepha, Josepha – (df) Yosef; God will increase יוֹסִיפָה

Yuta, Yute – (df) Yehudah; Praised יוּטָא, יוּטֶע (יְהוּדִית)

Z

Zahavah – Golden זָהָבָה

Zefirah – Crown צְפִירָה

Zelda, Zelde – Rare זֶעלדַא, זֶעלדֶע

Zelma, Selma – (df) Solomon; Peace זֶעלמַא, זֶעלמֶע

Zemirah – Song of joy זְמִירָה

Zerizah – Weary זְרִיזָה

Zilpah – Dropping זִלְפָּה

Zissel, Zissil – (df) Eliezer; God aids, sweet זִיסֶעל, זִיסִיל

Zissela, Zissele – (df) Eliezer; God aids, sweet זִיסְלָא, זוּסְלֶע

Ziva – Splendor, brightness זִיוָה

Zivanah – Light זִיוָנָה

Zlote – (df) Lotte, Charlotte – Strong (Teut.) זלאטֶע

"LET ME BE MY NAME UNTIL I MAKE MY NAME"
TENNYSON

Most names can be traced to their original meaning. They are derived from words and phrases of ancient languages, which can be defined like any other word.

In ancient times names were selected in association with one's characteristics or circumstances of birth. Thus, we find Adam, meaning "formed of red earth"; Abigail, meaning "her father's joy"; Aaron, "he who is exalted"; and Joshua, "the Lord is salvation."

But not everyone was given a new name. For it eventually became the custom to name people after biblical historical characters.

After many duplications of names a surname or family name came into existence. These were usually derived from local surroundings, trades, occupations, ancestral homes, and nicknames. Thus Joshua-son-of-Samuel became known simply as Joshua Cohen.

The derivations and definitions of names are compiled from authentic etymological sources; but some authorities disagree as to origins and meanings.

The study of names is an interesting art but it cannot be considered an exact science. Therefore, although your name means something you disapprove of, it becomes important to you alone and it is your personality that creates the true meaning. It can mean exactly what you want it to.

It is a good idea to select a name carefully, since one usually lives with it for the rest of his life.

If the child is born blonde, you would try not to name him something meaning "dark of complexion." Or if the physical heritage in your family is tall stature, you would avoid a name which means 'small and gentle."

Given Names of Males and Females and Their Meanings

ABBREVIATIONS

Ar	ARABIC		N	NORMAN
A	ARAMAIC		OE	OLD ENGLISH
C	CELTIC		OF	OLD FRENCH
D	DUTCH		P	PERSIAN
E	ENGLISH		R	RUSSIAN
F	FRENCH		S	SAXON
Gael	GAELIC		Scot	SCOTTISH
G	GREEK		Sl	SLAVONIC
H	HEBREW		Sp	SPANISH
Ir	IRISH		Sy	SYRIAC
I	ITALIAN		T	TEUTONIC
L	LATIN		W	WELSH

A NAME FOR A BOY

A

Aaron, Aron (H)—Lofty mountain
Abbott (H) — Father; ruler of an abbey
Abel (H)—Vanity; ephemeral
Abner (H)—Father of light
Abry—meaning uncertain
Adam (H)—Formed of red earth
Adlai (H)—Until me
Adolph (T) — Noble world; noble helper
Adrian (Gr)—Manly; brave
Alan, Allan (Gael)—He who is fast, majestic, and graceful; a hunting dog
Alban (L)—Fair
Albert (T)—Noble, bright; famous

Alen, Allen (L)—Cheerful
Alex, Alexander, Alexis (Gr) — Helper of men
Alfred (S)—All is peace (T)—Elf counseled
Alison, Allison (T)—Of holy fame
Alvan, Alvin (S)—Completely successful (T)—Beloved by all
Amos (H)—Burden bearer; strong; vigorous
Anatole (Gr)—Rising of the sun
Andrew, Andy (Gr)—Angelic
Archibald, Archie (T) — Bold; valiant; daring
Arlen, Arlin (C)—A pledge
Armand, Armin (T) — Commander of an army

Arnd, Arno, Arnold (T) — Eagle power (S)—Faithful to his honor
Art, Arthur, Artie (W)—Strong as a bear (Gr)—Noble; exalted
Aubrey (T)—Fair-haired chief (S) —Rich and mighty
Austin (L) — Imperial; renowned; royal
Avery (S)—Ruler of elves

B

Baldwin (T)—Prince friend; speedy conqueror
Banet, Barnet, Barnett, Barney (H) —Son of consolation
Barnard—See Bernard
Barrett (T)—Bear-like
Barrie, Barry (C)—Straight looker; straightforward
Bart, Barton (S) — A homestead (E)—Homeloving
Basil (G)—Kingly; royal
Bayard (T)—With red-brown hair
Bela (H)—Eloquent
Ben, Benjamin, Benson (H)—Son of the right hand
Benedict (L)—Blessed; wishing all good
Bennett—See Benedict
Bernard, Berni, Bernie (T)—Bold as a bear (S) Childlike; innocent
Bert, Berthold (T) — Bright; firm (S) A ruler
Bertram, Bertran, Bertrem (S) — Fair and pure (T)—Bright raven
Bill, Billie—See William
Blair (E)—Plain dweller
Bob, Bobbie, Bobby—see Robert
Boris (R)—Fight
Boyd (C)—Yellow haired
Brad, Bradford, Bradley (OE) — Broad form (of a stream); meadow
Brand, Brandon (T) — A flaming sword, firebrand
Brent (OE)—From the steep hill
Brett (C) — A Breton
Brian (C)—Strong (Gael)—Well-born (F)—Having a thundering voice
Brice, Bryce (C)—Quick moving
Bruce (Scot) — Happy conqueror (F) — From bruys, a place in Normandy
Bruno (T)—Brown
Bryan, Byron (E)—Clear discerner (T)—The cottage

Burl, Burleigh, Burley (T)—From the meadow by the hill or castle
Burnett (E)—The brown
Burt, Burton (T)—Fine
Byron (T)—From the cottage

C

Calvin (L)—Bald
Carl, Carlton (T)—Strong; manly
Carey, Cary (W)—Rocky island
Carol, Carrol, Caryl (T) — Man (L)—Praise
Cassius, Cass (L) — Vain
Cecil (L)—Blind; dim-sighted
Cedric (C)—Chieftain
Charles (T) — Of great strength; manly
Chester (L)—A camp
Clark (E) — Clerk; clergyman; scholar
Claude (E)—Lame
Clement (L)—Mild-tempered; gentle; merciful
Clifford (S)—Valorous
Clinton (T)—From the farm
Clive (S)—A cliff
Conrad (T)—Wise counsellor
Cornelius, Cornell, Cory (L) — The cornel tree
Craig (Gael)—A rock or stone
Curt, Curtis (OF)—Courteous
Cyril (T)—Splendor
Cyrus (P)—The sun

D

Dale (S)—A small valley
Dan, Daniel, Danny (H)—Judge of God; God is my judge
Dana (E)—Arbiter
Darren (E)—Darling
David (H)—Beloved
Dean (L)—Leader
Denis, Dennis (G)—From Dionysos, god of wine and drama
Devon—meaning uncertain
Dick, Dicky—See Richard
Don, Donald, Donn, Donnie, Donny (C)—Proud chief
Dore, Dorian, Dorie (G)—Golden
Douglas (Gael)—Dark; swarthy
Drew (E)—Adept, gifted
Dwight (T)—White or fair

E

Earl, Earle (E)—A title of nobility
Eben (H)—Relatives

Ed, Edd, Eddie, Eddy, Edward (T) —Happy guard; guardian of happiness

Edgar (T) — Good spearman; successful in war (S)—Honored; he who fulfills his promise

Edmund (S) — Blessed peace; defender of happiness

Edsel (T)—Rich

Edwin (S) — Happy conqueror (T) —Rich friend

Egan, Egon (C) — Ardent (Gr) — Strong handed

Eli, Elias, Elihu, Elijah, Ellis, Ely (H) — God is the Lord; God is exalted

Eliot, Elliot, Elliott—see Eli (W)— A huntsman

Ellery, Elroy (E)—Like the tree

Elmer (S)—Noble; bright

Elvin (T)—Godly friend

Emanuel, Emmanuel (H)—God with us

Emeric, Emeri, Emery, Emory (T) — Industrious (S) — Ever rich or mighty

Emil (T)—Industrious

Emmet (S) — An ant (possibly implying industry)

Eric (T)—Mighty lord; hero (S)— Brave; powerful

Ernest, Ernie, Ernst (S) — Zealous; serious (T)—Eagle king

Errol (L)—Traveler

Erwin, Erwyn (S) — A victorious lord, master, or soldier (W) — Very fair; white

Estes (L, Gr)—Italian place name

Ethan (H)—Strength; power

Eugene, Eugine (G)—Well born

Evan, Evans (C)—Young warrior (W)—Form of John

Everard, Everett, Evertt (T) — Strong as a wild boar (S)—Ever honored

F

Fabian (L)—Bean grower; cultivator

Fane (T)—Joyful

Farrel, Farrell (Ar) — A burden bearer

Felix (L)—Happy

Ferdinand, Ferdynand (T)—Daring; valiant; quick of comprehension

Floyd (W)—Brown, gray, hoary.

Foster (T)—Of the woodland

Francis (T) — Free; indomitable courage and strength

Frank—See Francis

Franklin, Franklyn (T)—A freehold farmer

Fred, Freddy, Frede, Frederic, Frederick, Fredric, Fredrick (T) — Peaceful ruler

G

Garnet (S)—Learned; skillful (T)— —Highly honored

Garry, Gary (Gael)—Brave spearman

Gaston (T)—Hospitable

Gene (C)—White sea of foam

Gentry—meaning uncertain

Geoffrey (T) — Joyful peace (S) — He who delights in peace

George (G) — A farmer; husbandman

Gerald, Gerard (T) — Powerful spearman

Gilbert (T)—Bright pledge

Gilford (S)—Kind and generous disposition

Glen, Glenn (Gael)—A small valley

Gordon (Gael)—A fine man (W)— A strong man

Gregory (G)—Watchman; vigilant

Gunter, Gunther (S)—Warrior

Gus, Gustave (T) — Staff of war; God's staff

Guy (F)—The mistletoe; also guide; leader; director

H

Hadley (OE)—From the heath meadow

Hal (T)—Healthy

Hans (S)—A free market or hall (T)—Form of John

Harlan, Harley, Harlin, Harmon (T) —Land of warriors

Harold (T)—Leader of the army

Harris, Harry—See Henry

Harrison—Son of Henry

Harvey, Harvie (C)—Bitter (T)— Noble soldier

Hayden (T)—Dweller on the hill

Hayward (T)—Guard of the hedge

Haywood, Heywood (T)—The wood within the hedges

Hector (Gr)—Defender

Helmut—meaning uncertain

Henry (T) — Home ruler (S) — Brave, powerful lord; wealthy

Herbart, Herbert (S)—Glory of the army (T)—Illustrious ruler

Herman (S)—Soldier; army man

Hilary, Hillard, Hillary, Hilliard (L) —Cheerful; merry; gay

Horace (L)—Light of the sun; keen-eyed

Howard (T) — Keeper of a hall; keeper of a stronghold

Hubert (T) — Bright mind (S) — Bright color

Hugh (S)—Thought

Hunt, Hunter (T) — A search; huntsman

I

Ian (Gael)—Form of John

Ike, Isaac (H)—Laughter

Ilerdon—meaning uncertain

Ionel—meaning uncertain

Ira, Iran (H)—City watch; watchful

Irvin, Irving (S)—Sea friend

Irwin, Irwing (H)—See Erwin

Isidor, Isadore, Isidore (G)—Strong gift; gift of Isis

Ivan (R, W)—Form of John

Ivar, Iver, Ivor (Scot)—Strong

J

Jac, Jack, Jackie—See John

Jaimie, James, Jamie, Jimmy (H) — The supplanter

Jan (D)—Form of John

Jared (H)—Descent

Jason, Jay (T)—Happy

Jean—See John

Jed (A)—Hand

Jeff, Jeffery, Jeffre, Jeffrey (S)—Joyful peace

Jerald, Jerold, Jerome, Jerry (H) — Exalted; placed high above others (Gr)—Holy fame

Jeremiah, Jeremy, Jerry (H) — Exalted of the Lord

Jess, Jesse (H)—Wealthy; also, the Lord exists

Job (H)—One who mourns; persecuted man

Jock (H)—God's gracious gift

Joda, Jody (L)—Playful

Joel (H) — He who wills or commands

John, Jon (H)—The Lord's grace

Jolan (L)—Cheerful

Jonah, Jonas (H)—A dove

Jorah, Jorey (H)—Autumn rain

Josiah (H)—The fire of the Lord; to whom the Lord is salvation

Judd (H) — One who is praised; praise the Lord

Jules, Julian, Julius (L)—Soft-haired; down-bearded (G)—Youthful

Justin, Justus (L) — Just; righteous; upright

K

Kay (E)—Strong; determined

Karl—See Carl

Keith (Gael)—A windy place (W) —An enclosed place; deep hollow

Kenneth, Kent (C) — Comely; a noble kind man

Kevin (Gael)—Handsome

Kin (W)—Leader; chief

Konrad—See Conrad

Kurt (T)—Able in counsel

L

Lance, Lancelot (L) — Servant, so called from carrying a lance or spike

Lane (OE)—A country road

Larry, Laurence, Lawrance, Lawrence, Lazarus (L) — Laurel-crowned

Lee, Leigh (T)—A pasture; meadow (S) — Sheltered place (W) — A stream

Leland (OE)—From meadow land

Lenard, Lennie, Leo, Leon, Leonard (L)—A lion; lion-hearted

Leopold (T) — Beloved and brave; defender of the people

Leroy (F)—The king

Leslie (T)—Low meadow (S)—A lessee

Lester (S)—Lustrous, possibly from Leicester, meaning meadow-camp

Lewis (S)—Safeguard of the people (T)—Illustrious warrior

Lindsay, Lindsey (E)—Mild (T)—By the sea.

Lion, Lionel, Lyonel (L)—Little lion

Lloyd (W)—Brown; gray

Lon, Lonnie (T)—Friend of all

Loren (L)—The Lost

Lou, Louis (F)—Form of Lewis

Lowell, Lovell (T)—Beloved

Ludwig (T)—Safeguard of the people; a good leader

Luke (L)—Light
Lyle (F, L)—From the island
Lynn (Gael)—A pool or lake

M

Macey, Macy—See Matthew
Malcolm (Gael) — The brown of a rock; a bald head (C)—A servant of Columba
Manfred (T)—Man of peace
Mannie, Manuel, Manny (H)—God with us
Marc, Marcus, Mark (L) — Polite; polished; brilliant; born in the month of March
Marlin—A form of Mary
Marshal, Marshall (T) — Commander; master of the house
Martin (L)—Martial; warlike
Marvin (Gael) — A ridge of very high hills
Matthew, Matty (H)—Reward; recompense; gift of the Lord
Maurice (L)—Dark of complexion; Moorish
Max, Maxwell (Gael)—Little son
Melvin, Melvyn (C)—Chieftain
Meredith, Merritt (W) — Admiral; protector of the sea
Merril (T)—Famous
Merwin, Merwyn—See Irvin
Michael, Mickey, Mike (H)—Who is like God
Miles, Myles (L)—A soldier
Milo (Gr)—A mighty wrestler
Milton (S) — Mill-town or middle-town (OE)—Mill farmstead
Mitchel, Mitchell (S) — A big man; possibly a variation of Michael
Moe, Moses, Moss (H) — Drawn from the water
Monroe (C)—From a mount on the river Roe
Monte, Monty (L)—Mountain
Mordi, Mordy, Morton, Morty (Gael)—Great hill
More, Morey, Morie, Morre, Morry, Murray, Murry (Gael) — Great water
Morel, Morrell, Morril, Morrill (L) —Swarthy
Moritz, Moriz—meaning uncertain
Morris—See Maurice
Mortimer (N)—Norman place name (C)—Sea warrior
Myron (Gr)—Myrrh

N

Nat, Nathan, Nathaniel (H) — Gift of God
Neal, Neil (C)—Champion (Gael) — Of a dark or swarthy complexion
Ned, Neda (T) — A need; Sabbath born
Nelson (E)—Living in Neil
Newton (OE) — From the new estate
Nicholas, Nicolas (Gr) — People's victory
Noah (H)—Rest; consolation; peace
Nolan, Noland (C) — Noble or famous
Norbert (OE) — Norse sea god; good cheer
Norman, Norton (T) — Man of the north; native of Normandy
Norris (T) — Man from the north (OF, L)—Caretaker

O

Oliver (L)—The olive
Oran, Orin (C)—White skin
Orie (H)—Light
Orson (L)—Bear
Oscar (C) — Bounding warrior; he who leaps to the fight
Osias (H) — Derived from Joshua; God will help you
Oswald (T)—Divine power
Otto (T)—Wealthy
Owen (C)—Young warrior
Orland (T) — Fame of the land; a form of Ronald

P

Parker (E)—Park keeper
Pat (L)—Noble or patrician
Paul (G)—Small; gentle
Pearce (F)—Perceptive
Percival, Percy (C) — Very courteous
Perry (OE)—A rock
Pete, Peter (Gr)—A stone
Philip, Phillip (Gr) — Lover of horses
Phineas (S) — An open and trusty countenance
Pier, Pierre (F)—Form of Peter
Preston (OE)—Clergy

R

Raleigh (OE)—Deer
Ralph, Randell (T)—Form of Randolph (OE)—House wold
Ramon, Ray, Raye, Raymond (T)— Wide protection; quiet, peaceful (T)—Strong man
Rand, Randey, Randolph, Randy (T) — Shielded by the wolf-god (S)—Pure, disinterested help
Raphael (H)—Healing of God
Regan (C)—Noble man
Reginald (T)—Powerful, judgment
Rex (L)—King, leader
Richard, Ricky (C)—Stern king (S) —Generous; benevolent; liberal
Rip, Ripley (S)—The shouter
Robert, Robin (T)—Bright in counsel
Robin (OE)—Good
Rod (T)—Winner over all
Rodger, Roger (T)—Spear of fame; strong in counsel
Rodney (T)—Famous in counsel
Rodolph—See Randolph
Roland (T) — The country's glory (S)—Counsellor to his country
Roman, Romie—meaning uncertain
Ronald, Ronnie, Ronny (S) — Worthy of admiration
Ronan (C)—A seal; a pledge
Rory, Roy, Roye (F)—A king (C) —Red
Ross (T) — A horseman; knight; chevalier; gallant
Rowland (T)—Fame of the land
Ruby (L)—A red precious stone
Rudolph, Rudy—See Randolph
Russ, Russel, Russell (F) — Red-haired

S

Sam, Samuel (H)—Asked of God
Samson (H)—Brilliant sun
Sandy—See Alexander
Sanford (E)—By the road
Saul (H)—Asked of the Lord
Scott (Scot)—Tattered
Sebastian (Gr)—Reverenced; venerable; honorable
Selwyn (Gr)—Royal friend
Serge (R) — Favorite Roman and medieval name
Seth (H)—Appointed
Seymore, Seymour, Sy (S) — A tailor

Shelby (E)—Farm dweller
Sheldon (OE)—Shepherd's hut
Shelley (T)—Shell island
Shepard, Shepherd (S)—A shepherd
Sherman (S)—A shearer, or cuts
Sherwin (OE)—Swift runner
Sherwood (S) — A clearing in the woods
Sidney, Sydney — Derived from St. Denis
Siegfried, Siggi (T) — Victorious peace
Sigmond, Sigmund (T) — Victorious peace; man of victory
Simeon—See Simon
Simon (H) — Hearing and obeying; attentive
Sol, Sollie, Solomon (H) — Peaceful
Spencer (F) — A steward; dispenser to a large household
Stanford (S)—From the stone
Stanley, Stanton (OE) — Meadow dweller
Stefan, Stephen, Steve, Steven (Gr) —A crown or garland
Steward—See Stuart
Stuart (T)—A steward; waiter; one who has charge of a place
Sylvan (L)—Forest

T

Ted, Tedd, Teddy — See Edward and Theodore
Terence (L)—Soft or tender
Terry (L)—Beloved leader
Theodore (Gr)—Gift of God; divine gift
Thomas, Tom, Tommy (A, H)—A twin
Tibor (L)—From the River Tiber
Timothy (Gr)—Honoring God
Tobias, Toby (H) — Goodness of God
Todd (E)—Thick foliage
Tracy (S)—The brave
Ty, Tyler (E) — Maker of tiles or bricks

U

Uland, Ulen (T) — From the noble land
Ulom (H)—Strong
Ulrich (T) — Noble ruler (S) — A powerful or rich helper

V

Van (T)—Advance
Victor (L)—A conqueror

W

Wade (D)—A meadow or pasture
Wallace (Gael)—From Wales
Walter (T) — Chief of an army; woodmaster
Warner (T)—A protecting warrior
Warren (T)—Protecting friend
Wayne (OE)—A wagon-maker
Wendell (D)—A walker or traveler (T)—Wandering
Wesley (OE)—Of west meadow
Wilbert, Wilbur (S)—Wild boar

Wilfred (S)—Peaceful
Willard, William, Willis (T)—Defender; protector of many; shield
Winfred (T)—Friend or winner of peace
Woodrow (OE)—From near forest

Y

Yale (W)—Welsh place name
York, Yorke—Yew tree

Z

Zachary (H) — Whom the Lord remembers
Zane (L)—Form of John
Zolto—meaning uncertain

A NAME FOR A GIRL

A

Abbey (S) — Sweet refuge; also a form of Abigail
Abigail (H)—Her father's joy
Ada (T)—Happy (H)—Ornament, significant of great beauty
Adaline, Adda, Addie, Adela, Adelaide, Adele, Adeline, Adelle, Adia, Adie, Adine (T) — Noble maiden (S) — Descended from nobles
Adolphine (T) — Noble wolf; good luck name
Adria, Adrian, Adriene, Adrienne (L)—Black earth; peat soil
Agnes (Gr) — Pure; chaste; honorable
Aileen—See Helen
Aimee, Amy (L, F)—Beloved
Alberta (T)—Noble; bright
Alexandra, Alexis (Gr) — Helper of mankind
Alfreda (S) — All peace (T) — Elf counseled
Alice (S)—Noble; illustrious
Alma (L)—Fair
Alua, Aludra (T)—A virgin
Amelia (Gr)—Busy
Anabelle, Annabel (H, L) — Beautiful Ann
Andrea (L)—Proud
Ann, Anna, Anne, Annie (H) — Grace; gracious; merciful
Anita, Annette (H, L) — Little, charming Ann
April (L)—The fourth month; open

Arleen, Arlene, Arline, Arlyne (R) A pledge
Audrey (E)—Threatener; illustrious; august; golden (T)—Noble

B

Barbara, Bobby, Bobie (Gr) — A stranger; foreign
Beatie, Beatrice (L)—Blessed; happy
Bela, Bella, Belle (L)—Beautiful
Belinda (I) — Serpent; graceful in motion
Berenice, Bernice (Gr) — She who brings victory
Berta, Bertha, Berthe, Bertina (S)— Bright; famous
Beryl (Gr)—A crystal
Bess, Bessie, Betsy, Bette, Bettina, Betty — From Elizabeth (L) — Blessed (H)—Oath of God
Beth (H)—House or home
Beulah (H)—Married
Beverle, Beverley, Beverly (S) — Beaver meadow
Birdie — A modern name, suggesting bird-like qualities
Blanch, Blanche (F) — White; fair; beautiful
Blossom (OE)—A flower
Bona, Bonita, Bonnie, Bonny (L) — Good; fair
Brenda (T)—A sword (C)—Dark-haired; dark-eyed
Bridget (C) — Strength (Gael) — Fiery dart

C

Camellia, Camilla, Camille (L) — Servant of the people
Candy (Gr)—White
Carla, Carol, Carole, Carrie, Carroll, Cary, Caryl (T) — Strong; valiant
Carmen (L) — Song; also signifies a charm
Caroline, Carolyn (T) — Valiant; strong
Catherine, Cathleen, Cathy (Gr) — Pure; virtuous
Cecila, Cecile, Cecily (L)—Lover of harmony
Cecilia, Cecilie, Cecillie, Cele (L) —Gray-eyed
Celeste, Celestine (L)—Heavenly
Celia, Celina, Celine (Gr) — One who commands
Charlene (T)—Strong
Charlet, Charlot, Charlotte (T) — Noble-spirited
Cherie (F)—Dear one
Cheryl (E)—Courageous
Claire (F)—Form of Clara
Clara, Clare, Clarissa, Claryce (L) —Shining; glorious; brilliant; clear
Claudette, Claudia (L)—From Claudius, meaning lame
Colleen (R)—A maid; girl
Connie, Constance (L) — Steadfast; firm; unyielding
Cora, Coral, Corinna (Gr) — A maiden
Corinne (Gr)—A maiden
Cornelia (L) — Horn, the symbol of kingship
Cynthia (Gr) — Another name for Diana; from Mt. Cynthus

D

Daisy (S)—The eye of the day; the daisy is a symbol of innocence
Dale (S)—A small valley
Dana (L)—Bright
Daphne (Gr)—A laurel or bay tree
Darlene (S)—Darling
Daryl, Darryl (S)—As darling
Deanne (L)—Bright
Deborah, Debra (H)—A bee; industrious; active
Deena, Dena, Denna—See Dinah
Delilah (H)—Delicate

Denise (F)—Feminine form of Dennis
Desiree (F, L)—Beloved
Diana, Diane (L)—The moon; clear; bright; the goddess of hunting
Dinah (H) — She who is judged; vindicated
Dolly—See Dorothy
Dolores (Sp, L) — Sorrow
Donna (L)—Lady
Dora, Doreen, Dorene, Dorina—See Dorothy
Doris—See Dorothy
Dorothea, Dorothee, Dorothy (Gr) —Gift of God
Dulce (L)—Sweet

E

Edie, Edith, Edye, Edyth, Edythe (T) — Rich gift; happiness; prosperity
Edna, Ednah (H)—Pleasure
Edwina—Feminine form of Edwin
Eileen (Ir)—Form of Helen
Elaine, Elane, Elayne—See Helen
Eleanor, Elenor, Elinor—See Helen
Elisa, Elise, Elissa—See Elizabeth
Eliza, Elizabeth, Elize (H) — Oath of God
Ella (T)—Elf friend; also see Helen
Ellen, Ellin—See Helen
Eloise (T)—Famous holiness
Elsa, Else, Elsie (T) — Noble cheer; also a form of Alice or Elizabeth
Emily (L) — A worker; busy; energetic (Gr) — Of winning manners (S) — A nurse
Emma (T)—Grandmother; a nurse
Enid (C)—Soul
Erica—Feminine form of Eric
Essie, Estella, Estelle (F, L) — A star
Ester, Esther (P)—A star
Ethel (T)—Noble
Etta (T)—Home ruler
Eunice (Gr) — Happy victory; she who makes fortunate conquests
Eva, Eve (H) — A mother; life-giving
Eveline (C)—Pleasant
Evelyn (L) — Hazel nut (C) — Pleasant

F

Faith (L)—A firm believer
Fannie, Fanny—See Frances

Fay, Faye, Fayette (Sp)—Faith

Felice, Felicia (L) — Happy; fortunate

Fern (S) — The fern is a symbol of sincerity

Flora, Floren, Florette, Flossie (L) —A flower

Florence (L)—Flourishing; prosperous

Fran, Frances, Francine (T)—Free; indomitable courage and strength

Freda, Frederica, Fredrika, Freeda, Frieda (T)—Peaceful ruler

Frieda (T)—Peaceable

Frumet (H)—Religious

G

Gail, Gale—See Abigail

Gay (OF)—Loving pleasure; merry

Gene, Genevieve (C)—White sea of foam

Georgette, Georgia, Georgina—Feminine forms of George

Geraldene, Geraldine (T) — Spear power

Gerda (N, T) — Enclosed cornfield; an emblem of peace

Germaine (T)—Firm spear

Gerselle (T)—Heroine

Gertrude (T)—Spear maiden

Gilda (C)—Servant of God

Gladys (W)—Lame

Gloria (L)—Glorious

Golda, Goldie (T)—Golden haired

Grace (L) — Grace; kindness; patience (E)—God's blessing

Greta, Gretchen—See Margaret

Griselda (T)—Grey-eyed lady

Gussie (L)—Revered

Guta (Gr)—Good

Gwen, Gwendaline, Gwendolyn, Gwenne, Gwennie (C) — Whitebrowed

H

Hannah (H) — Gracious; merciful; benign

Harriet, Harriette, Hattie (T) — Home ruler (S) — Ever rich and powerful

Hazel (H)—One that sees God

Hedy—See Esther

Heidi (Swiss)—Country girl

Helaine, Helena, Helene (Gr) — Light

Helen (Gr) — Light; bright as the dawn

Helga (N)—Holy

Henney, Henrietta, Henriette (T)— Home ruler (S) — Ever rich or mighty

Hepzibah (H)—My delight is in her

Herma, Hermina (T)—Beloved

Hetty—See Esther

Hilda, Hildegarde (T)—Battle maid

Hinda (S)—Hind, deer

Honey (S)—Honey

Hope (S)—Trust in the future

Hortense (L)—Gardener

I

Ida, Idel (T)—Happy (C)—Thirsty

Ilene (Ir)—Bright

Ina (L)—Mother

Inez (Gr)—Pure

Irene (Gr) — Messenger of peace; peaceable

Iris (Gr)—A link of beauty uniting earth and sky; the rainbow

Irma (T)—Maiden of high degree

Isabel, Isabele, Isabella, Isabelle, Isobel (Sp)—Form of Elizabeth

Isidora (Gr)—A gift

J

Jacobina—Feminine of Jacob

Jacqueline (H)—Supplanter; beguiling

Jan, Jane, Janet, Janice, Janie, Janis —Derived from John (H) — The Lord's grace

Jean, Jeanne, Jeannette, Jennie, Jenny —See Jane

Jemima (H) — A dove; handsome as the day

Jessi, Jessica, Jessie (H)—Wealthy

Jewel (H)—Life (OF)—Joy

Jill (L)—Soft-haired

Joan, Joann, Joanna, Joanne, Johanna —See Jane

Jocelin, Jocelyn, Joscelind (L)—Just, honest

Jola, Jolan, Jolyn (OF)—Joyful

Josepha, Josephine (H) — She who shall increase

Joy, Joyce (L) — Gladness; cheerful, merry (OF)—Joyful

Judith, Judy (H)—She who praises

Julia, Juliana, Julie, Juliet (L)—Soft-haired

June (L)—Youthful

Justine (L)—Just; righteous

K

Karen (T)—Pure
Karolyn, Karyl (T)—Valiant
Kate, Katherine, Kathleen, Kay—See Catherine
Koka—meaning uncertain

L

Laura, Laurel, Lauren, Laurette, Laurie (L) — Laurel; the laurel is the emblem of fame
Lea, Leah, Lee (H) — Weary; exhausted
Leanne, Lena, Lenni, Lennie (Gr)—Light (L)—Peace, gentleness
Lenor, Lenora, Leonore (Gr)—Light (L)—Lion-like strength and courage
Leatrice—From Leah
Leigh (E)—Quiet
Leona, Leonie (G)—Strength
Leslie (T)—Low meadow
Letitia (L)—Joy or gladness
Libby (E)—Oath of God
Lila, Lilac, Lilah, Lilli, Lilian, Lillian, Lilly, Lily, Lilyan (L)—The lily is the symbol of purity (P)—flower
Line—See Caroline
Linda, Lynda (T) — Lovely maid; also see Belinda
Linn, Linne (W)—Cataract; lake
Lisa (E)—Oath of God
Lita—See Letitia
Lois (F)—Famous in battle
Lola (T)—Man
Lora, Loretta, Lori, Loria, Lorine—See Laura
Loraine, Lorraine (T) — Famous in war
Lotte, Lottie—See Charlotte
Louisa, Louise (F, S) — Protectress of the people
Lucia, Lucille, Lucy (L) — Light; born at daybreak
Lyda, Lydia (Gr) — With a good mind
Lynn, Lynne (Gael) — A pool or lake

M

Mabel (L) — Beloved; beautiful (F)—My belle, or fair one
Madeline—See Magdalene
Mae—See Mary

Magdalene (H) — A watch tower; elevated; magnificent
Mailda—See Matilda
Mala, Malina (H)—A tower
Malvina (C) — Handmaid (F) — Smooth-browed
Marcella, Marcia, Marcilen, Marsha, Marshe (L) — Martial; fearless; brave
Marcene (F)—Lovely
Mareea, Maria, Marian, Marie (H)—Bitterness
Margaret, Marge, Margery, Margot (Gr)—A pearl; precious; beautiful
Marietta (H)—Exalted
Margo, Marjorie, Marjory — See Margaret
Marilyn, Marleen, Marlene — Derived from Mary
Marion—See Mary
Marsha, Marshe—See Marcia (R)—Without fear
Martha (H) — Becoming bitter (A)—Mistress
Mary (H)—Distressed; tearful
Matilda (T)—A noble lady
Maureen—From Mary
Maxine (L) — Possibly from Maximus, meaning greatest
May (E) — Born in May (L) — Beloved (Gr)—Pearl
Mayda (T)—Olden form of maiden
Melanie (Gr)—Darkness
Melicent (Gr)—Sweet as honey (T)—Work strength
Melissa (Gr)—Honey-bee
Merle (F)—A blackbird
Michal, Michel, Michele, Michelle (H)—Who is like God
Mignon (F)—Darling; delicate
Mildred (T)—Mild of speech; gentle
Millicent—See Melicent
Millie, Milly (E)—Comforter
Mimi (T)—Martial
Mina, Minna (T) — Memory; beloved
Minerva (L)—Goddess of wisdom
Minnie, Minette (T) — Borne in memory; beloved
Miriam—See Mary
Mitzi—meaning uncertain
Mollie, Molly—See Mary
Mona, Monica (L)—Pure; counsel
Muriel (Gr)—Myrrh; perfume
Myra (Gr)—She who weeps; myrrh
Myrna (C)—Gentle

Myrtle (Gr)—The myrtle, sacred to Venus; beauty's crown

N

Nada (Sp)—Hope
Nadia (Sl)—Hope
Nadine (F)—Hope
Nan, Nanci, Nancy, Nanette — See Hannah
Naomi (H)—Good to look at; agreeable; pleasant
Natalie, Nathalie (L) — Birthday, lively
Nell, Nellie—See Eleanor
Nettie, Netty (G)—High esteem
Nina (Sp) — Little darling; also see Ann
Nora, Norah, Noreen (L) — Honor; also see Leonore
Norma (L)—A rule; model; standard

O

Olga (R, T)—Holy
Olive (L)—Peace
Opal, Ophelia (Gr)—Serpent; help-giver; useful

P

Pam, Pamela, Pamella (Gr) — All sweetness; a brunette; a song or melody
Pat, Patricia, Patsy, Patti (L) — Noble, patrician
Patience (L)—Bearing up; enduring affliction without complaint
Paula, Paulette, Pauline, Paulyn (F) —Little
Pearl, Perla (Gr)—A pearl
Peg, Peggy—See Margaret
Penelope, Penney, Pennie, Penny (Gr)—A weaver
Petra—Form of Peter
Phebe, Phoebe (Gr) — Radiant; splendid; the moon
Phillis, Phyllis (Gr) — Green leaf; bough
Pia (I)—Pious
Polly (H)—Bitter
Portia (L)—A harbor; safety
Priscilla (L) — Little; quaint; old-fashioned

R

Rachel, Rachelle (H)—Innocence
Rae, Raye—See Rachel

Reba, Rebecca (H)—A rope with a noose; a snare; a girl who ensnares men by her beauty
Reda, Reheta, Reitha, Rhieta, Rita—See Margaret
Regina (L)—A queen
Rene, Renea, Renee, Reina (L) — Renewed
Retta—See Henrietta
Rhea (Gr)—Protector
Rhoda (Gr)—A rose
Ricki, Rickie, Ricky—See Roberta
Rita (L)—A pearl
Roberta, Robertta, Robin (T) — Bright in counsel
Rochelle (L)—A small stone
Rona, Ronni, Ronnie (T)—Powerful ruler
Rosa, Rosalie, Rosalind, Rosaline, Rosalyn, Rosamond, Roselyn, Roslyn, Rosabel (L) — Fair as a rose
Rose (L)—The rose is a symbol of love
Ruby (L)—Red; the ruby betokens a contented mind
Ruth (H)—A vision of beauty

S

Sadie, Sallie, Sally—See Sara
Salome (H)—Peaceful
Samara—Form of Samuel
Sandra, Sandy, Sondra—From Alexandra or Cassandra
Saralyn — A combination of Sarah and Lynn
Saran, Sarann — A combination of Sarah and Ann
Seema, Sema (Gr)—Sprout
Seena—From Sinai
Selda (S)—Hut
Selina (C)—Fair as the moon
Selma (C)—Fair
Serefina—Derived from Sara
Serena (L)—Happy
Sharon—See Rose
Sheila, Sheilah, Sheilla, Shela, Shelley, Shelva—See Cecilia
Sheri—See Cheri
Sherry, Sheryl—See Cheryl
Shirlee, Shirley—From the meadow
Sibyl (Gr)—A prophetess; divinely inspired; wise woman
Sida, Sidi (Gr)—A water-lily
Silvia (L)—Of the forest
Siss—See Cecelia

Sonia, Sonya (Sl)—Wisdom (Gr)—Bright
Sophia, Sophie (Gr)—Wise woman
Stefanie, Stephanie (F) — Crown garland
Stella (L)—A star
Sue, Susan, Susanna, Susanne, Susette, Susie, Suzanne (H)—A lily
Sybil—See Sibyl
Sydel, Sydell, Sydelle (Gr)—A sibyl
Sylvia—See Silvia

T

Tamar, Tamara, Tamarah (H) — A palm tree; spice
Teresa—See Theresa
Thea (Gr)—Goddess
Thelma (Gr)—Nursling
Theodora, Theodoria (G) — Divine gift
Terry, Theresa, Therese (H) — Beautiful
Thyrza (H)—Pleasant; agreeable
Tilda, Tillie—See Matilda
Tina (T)—Grave; serious
Toni (L)—Graceful
Tosia—meaning uncertain
Tracy (S)—The brave
Trude—See Gertrude

U

Ulrica (T)—Rich
Una (L)—The one
Undine (L)—Watery
Urania (F)—Heavenly
Ursula (L)—Little she-bear

V

Valeria, Valerie (L)—Healthy
Vera (L)—Truth
Verna, Veronica (L)—True image
Vicki, Vicky, Victoria (L) — The victorious
Vida—Derived from David
Viola, Violet (L) — A violet; pretty and modest
Virgina, Virginia (L) — A virgin; chaste
Vivian, Vivien (L) — Lively; merry (W)—The small water

W

Wanda (T)—The wanderer
Wenda (W)—White; fair
Wendey, Wendy (E)—Adventurous
Wilhelmina, Wilma (T)—Protector of many; shield; defense

X

Xenia (Gr)—Hospitality

Y

Yetta (H)—Ruler
Yolanda, Yolande (L)—Strong
Yvette (F)—The archer
Yvonne (T) — Archer (H) — God's grace or gift

Z

Zea (L)—The grain
Zelda (T)—Battle heroine
Zelia (G)—The zealous
Zena, Zenith (C)—Woman
Zillah (H)—Restful
Zoe (L)—Life
Zora (Sl)—Dawn

Aliyah — "Going up." An honor given the worshiper, to recite the blessing over the Torah.

Ametz — adoption.

Ark — repository of Torah scrolls.

Avraham — Abraham.

Avram — Abram.

Ba-al Brit — The sandek is also known as the Ba-al Brit (Master of the Covenant).

Bar Mitzvah — At the age of thirteen a Jewish boy attains religious majority.

Beth Din — a court of three rabbis or laymen.

Brit — ritual circumcision.

Canaan — "Lowland," early name of Palestine.

Erev — eve of holyday.

Gaon — title of head of the early medieval rabbinical academies in Babylon. Adj., gaonic.

Ger — proselyte (one who desires to be admitted into the Jewish fold).

Gevatter (German) — godfather.

Gevatterin (German) — godmother.

Halakhah — the accepted law.

Hallah — white twist bread used on the Sabbath and holydays.

Hametz — "sour" food, not permitted on Passover.

Hatofat dam — to draw a drop of blood.

Hol-Hamoed — intermediate days of Passover and Tabernacles.

Hoshaanah Rabbah — seventh day of Succot.

Hoshaanot — songs of praise, on Succot.

Kiddush — benediction over cup of wine.

Kiddush Hashem — sanctification of God's name.

Kinnot — prayers of sadness, on fast days.

Kohen (kohanim) — one of priestly descent, given the first honor when the Torah is read.

Kos shel Eliyahu — the fifth goblet at the seder table, for the prophet Elijah.

Kosher — proper; food in accordance with Jewish dietary laws.

Lag B'Omer — thirty-third day in Omer.

Leḥuppah ulemaasim tovim — end of special prayer, "May you be privileged to raise your child for study of Torah, for marriage, and for the performance of good deeds."

Letorah — the special prayer, Misheberakh, asks that the child devote himself to Jewish learning.

Levi — the second portion of the Torah is assigned to one who traces his descent to the tribe of Levi.

Maariv — evening service.

Mazal Tov — good luck, congratulations.

Mezuzah — parchment scroll attached to doorpost.

Midrash — commentary and legendry on Bible text.

Mikvah — ritual pool.

Minḥah — offering; afternoon prayer.

Minyan — a quorum of ten men for public worship.

Mishnah — primary part of the Talmud, first code of Jewish Law.

Mitzvah — good deed.

Mohel — ritual circumciser.

Nidḥeh — put ahead, as a holyday.

Nisan — the first Hebrew month, in the spring.

Pesaḥ — Passover.

Pidyon Ha-Ben — redemption of the firstborn son.

Purim — Feast of Lots.

Rav — one of the great scholars of the Talmud.

Rosh Hodesh — New Moon.

Rosh Hashanah — the New Year; the two days are considered one long day.

Sandek — (derived from the word syndicus — a patron) an honor given the most respected member of the family, to hold the child at the brit.

Sanhedrin — high council of the Jews, supreme court.

Seder — ceremonial Passover meal.

Selaim — coins.

Seudah, Seudat — family dinner in home celebration.

Shabbat — Sabbath.

Shalom Zakhar — Peace, little boy.

Shekalim — plural of shekel.

Shekel — coin or weight.

Shema — "Hear, O Israel," opening word of the declaration of God's oneness.

Shemoneh Esreh — silent prayer, recited standing.

Shulḥan Arukh — code of laws.

Simḥah — joyous occasion.

Siyum Bekhorim — On the morning prior to the eve of Passover firstborn sons visit the synagogue and listen to completion of a tractate of the Talmud.

Succot — Feast of Booths.

Tabernacles — Feast of Booths.

Tallit — prayer shawl.

Tallit Katan — fringes, attached to the four corners of a small garment worn all day under the outer clothing.

Talmud — study; the published oral discussion and interpretation of Holy Writ.

Tishah B'Av — Ninth of Av (month).

Torah — the five books of Moses.

Tzaddik — righteous person.

Tzitzit — fringes attached to the four corners of the tallit.

Tzom Gedalyah — Fast of Gedaliah.

Yisrael — Israelite.

Yom Kippur — Day of Atonement.

Yom Tov — holyday.

Zakhar — male.

Zohar — kabbalistic interpretation of the Pentateuch.

"We Love These Little People,
and It Is No Small Thing
When They Who Are So Fresh From God Love Us."